THE CULTURE OF MIGRATION IN SOUTHERN MEXICO

The Culture of Migration in Southern Mexico

Jeffrey H. Cohen

UNIVERSITY OF TEXAS PRESS
Austin

Some of the material in chapter 5 appeared in 2002 as "Migration and 'Stay at Homes' in Rural Oaxaca, Mexico: Local Expression of Global Outcomes" in *Urban Anthropology* 31(1): 231–259.

Printed in the United States of America
First edition, 2004

♾ The paper used in this book meets the minimum requirements of ANSI/NISO Z39.48-1992 (R1997) (Permanence of Paper).

LIBRARY OF CONGRESS CATALOGING-IN-PUBLICATION DATA
Cohen, Jeffrey H. (Jeffrey Harris)
The culture of migration in Southern Mexico / by Jeffrey H. Cohen. — 1st ed.
p. cm.
Includes bibliographical references and index.
ISBN 0-292-70570-0 (cl. : alk. paper) —
ISBN 0-292-70592-1 (pbk. : alk. paper)
1. Oaxaca (Mexico : State)—Emigration and immigration.
2. Migration, Internal—Mexico—Oaxaca (State) 3. United States—Emigration and immigration. I. Title.
JV7409.A20293 2004
304.8'0972'74—dc22 2004001007

CONTENTS

ACKNOWLEDGMENTS

Sometimes projects jump out at us. Studying migration was like that for me—it was a subject of serious conversations in rural communities and large cities in Oaxaca. Everyone talked about it, and everyone had an opinion. I was lucky enough to be able to investigate migration in Oaxaca and as it came alive in the actions and activities of the people around me. It is my hope that this presentation and analysis of my findings in some way illuminates what was going on in Oaxaca's central valleys from the late 1990s through the start of the twenty-first century.

The study of Mexican migration in Oaxaca tends to focus on ethnographic case studies—in other words, the story of migration in specific communities. Such work is extremely important, but ethnographic studies can create problems. A focus on individual communities comes at the expense of defining regional outcomes and understanding regional patterns. Given the many contradictory viewpoints I had heard concerning Oaxacan migration, I wanted to accomplish a few different goals. First, I wanted to define the history of movement for the central valleys as a way to counter the assumption that migration is rooted in recent changes and developments. Second, I wanted to follow migration throughout the valleys to get a better sense of how communities vary. Third, I wanted to place that movement into a broader framework for the comparative understanding of migration. The result is in your hands and describes what I define as a "culture migration" in Oaxaca.

To understand contemporary patterns of migration and to follow its historical development, I combined traditional research tools in a less than traditional setting. I worked in many communities, with a large team of fieldworkers; we conducted surveys and layered on participant observation where we could. We sought to examine migration in detail across a large sample of communities—twelve in all. In the process, we lost some of the depth and ethnographic richness that would come with a more detailed study of one community. On the other hand, and as I believe this text bears out, we discovered patterns that extend well beyond the limits of a single place.

This study began in 1996, with a summer in Santa Ana del Valle, Tlacolula, Oaxaca, a Zapotec-speaking pueblo I documented in *Cooperation and Community* (Cohen 1999). The pilot I administered sought to understand patterns of migration in the village over time and the outcomes of migrant decision making and remittance flows for villagers living in Santa Ana.

The project expanded in 1999 when I was awarded a CAREER grant from the National Science Foundation (BCS-9875539). The study grew from 2000 through 2003, and I have benefited from additional support provided by two graduate supplements and one undergraduate supplement to my original National Science Foundation grant. A Hewlett Faculty Developing Country Research Initiation Grant provided new support and new opportunities in 2002, and the Global Fund from the College of the Liberal Arts at Pennsylvania State University allowed me to present results of this work at the inaugural conference of the Academy for Migration Studies in Denmark (AMID). I continue to work on the project and plan for additional fieldwork in 2004 with the support of a Fulbright–García Robles award.

A study this large does not happen without a great deal of help and support at a personal and institutional level. When I began this work, I was a member of the faculty at Texas A&M University, and their support allowed me to conduct the pilot work for this project in 1996. In 2000, I joined the faculty at the Pennsylvania State University, where the Department of Anthropology, the Population Research Center, the program in demography, and the College of the Liberal Arts have all contributed to my continued success. In Oaxaca, none of this work would have been possible without the support of the Instituto Tecnológico de Oaxaca—my home away from home.

Just as important have been the many individuals in the United States and Mexico who have contributed support, energy, and friendship throughout this work. First, I want to thank the many Oaxacans who opened their homes to my team. *Presidentes municipales* and their fellow officers allowed us to work in their villages and often took time out of their busy schedules to answer specific questions concerning community histories. In households, we asked for about an hour of time to complete our survey, and often we stayed much longer. That so many people patiently answered our queries and then often spent additional time letting us probe their lives continues to amaze me. There is no way I can express how grateful I am.

The success of this work is also based in efforts of colleagues, friends, and students in the United States and Mexico. Two people in particular helped make this project a success, and I hope they know how much their friendship, support, and critical judgment means. Without Dr. Sylvia Gijon Cruz and Dr. Rafael Reyes Morales, this project would have taken far longer to complete, and it would have been far more frustrating. They were with me through each step of this project, both joined me in surveys, and together we conducted the research.

Many students worked with me throughout this project. In Mexico, I am indebted to Miguel, Erma, Salvador (Chava), Guadalupe, Paty, Jesus, Jorge, and Bersain. At Penn State, I have had the pleasure of working with graduates and undergraduates throughout this project. Undergraduate students who joined me and participated in fieldwork include Elisa Huerta, Abigail Renden, and Amos Gardner. With additional support from the National Science Foundation, two students, Maria Puente and Margaret Fox, conducted a short study in 2002 that supplemented my efforts and focused on the changes in the way women organize their kitchens. One of the highlights of working with Maria and Maggie was watching them win second prize in the social sciences in a university-wide competition held at Penn State. Malena Vinocur also helped with data entry for my research, and finally, Leila Rodriguez spent many hours cleaning and organizing the data. Her efforts as my research assistant over the last two years have made this project much more manageable, and for that I am thankful.

I am blessed with great friends and colleagues who are always ready to talk and who have helped me work through many issues. There are so many people that I am afraid I have likely forgotten at least a few, but I do want to say thanks to the members of the "Oaxaca Mafia," which includes (but is not limited to) Martha Rees, Jayne Howell, Michael Chibnik, Ron Waterbury, Arthur Murphy, William Wood, and Stephen Tulley. Also, thanks to Tad Matersbaugh, Lisa Cliggett, Richard Wilk, Paul Durrenburger, Dennis Conway, Robert Dover, Russ Bernard, Garry Chick, Gordon De Jong, Leif Jensen, Jacqueline Toribio, and Sal Oropesa. I also want to thank Lillian Traeger and the folks who participated in the annual meeting of the Society for Economic Anthropology in 2003. The topic was migration, and the weekend helped me work through several issues. This is my second book with the University of Texas Press, and I remain extremely grateful to Theresa May and her amazing staff for their support and effort in this project. Finally, to Maria, Max, and Annabelle, thanks for letting me leave for summer fieldwork and putting up with my rants and raves throughout the writing process. When I finished my dissertation research in 1993, I promised Maria that I would start working in a place where clean water was a little easier to find and the dust wasn't quite so thick. I guess I lied—ten years later, I am still in Oaxaca. I just can't seem to get it out of my head.

THE CULTURE OF MIGRATION IN SOUTHERN MEXICO

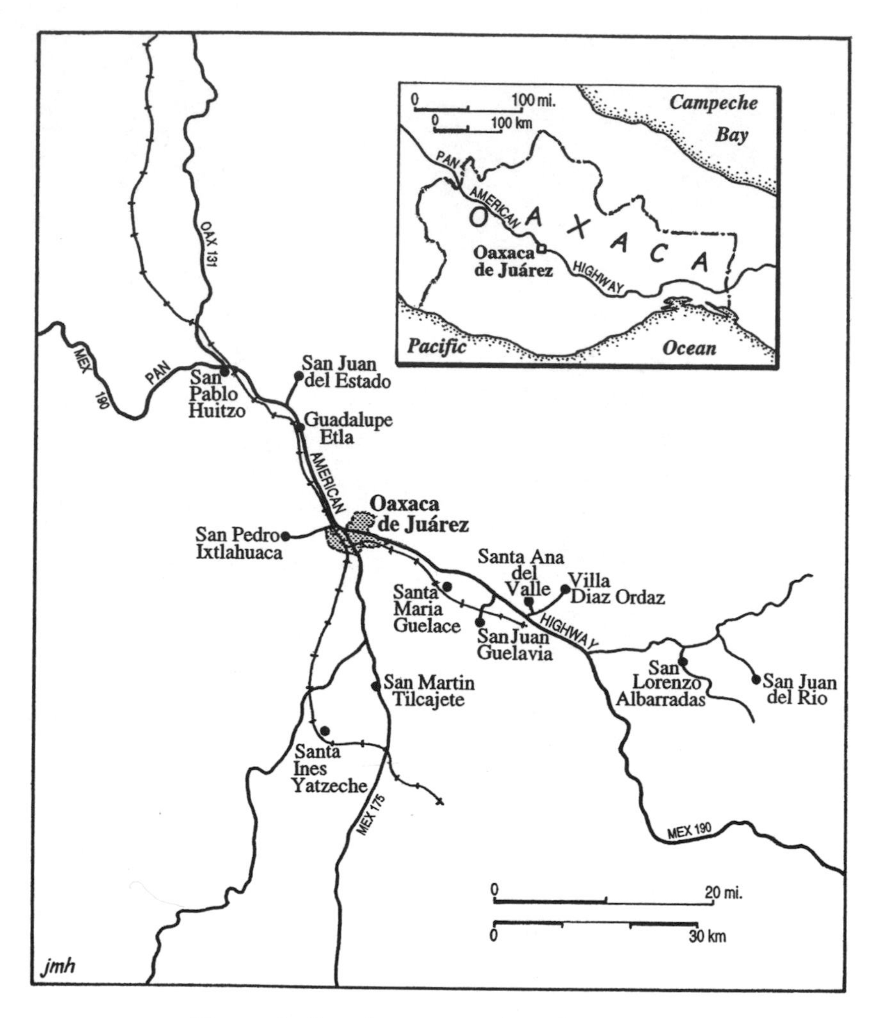

The central valleys of Oaxaca. Map by Michael Hollingsworth.

Introduction STUDYING MIGRATION IN OAXACA'S CENTRAL VALLEYS

There are many ways to approach the study of migration. In this ethnography of migration in the central valleys of Oaxaca, Mexico (the intermontane region surrounding the state's capital), I will argue that a cultural model—that is, a model in which the decision to migrate is rooted in the everyday experiences of rural Oaxacans—is most useful. However, before I describe that model, I want to begin by offering two views of migration that come from two Mexican folk songs. The first is "Llegan los norteños" ("The Norteños Arrive"), by Guillermo Velázquez y los Leones de la Sierra de Xichú (García de León 2003). The song tells the story of migrants from the north of Mexico who move from their hometowns to cities in the United States in an effort to find wage labor. The refrain, from which the title is taken, establishes the daunting nature of the Norteño's lot:

> Llegan los norteños masticando inglés, vuelvan a la fiesta, vuelvan a su tierra.
> Se acaba la fiesta y a sigue la guerra, en busca del dólar se van otra vez.
> [Here come the Norteños, chewing up English, they return for the fiesta, they return to their homeland.
> Once the fiesta is finished, the war continues, looking for dollars, they go again.][1]

The Norteño's life is a never-ending process of movement across borders that are both geographic and social. He (the Norteño is typically a young man) does not learn English well enough to integrate fully into the U.S. system. At the same time, the urge to find well-paid work means he cannot stay in Mexico. The Norteño lives by moving between Mexico and the United States. He returns to Mexico, but only for fiestas and brief visits with family. Then he must again cross the border to continue the "battle," seeking out dollars.

The second example contrasts with Velázquez's song and comes from "Canción mixteca," by José López Alvaréz. Described as an "achingly beautiful anthem of the lonely Mixtec farmworker" (Magagnini 2002), "Song of the Mixtec" tells of the longing that the Mixtecos, a minority population in the state of Oaxaca, feel for their homeland when they are abroad.

> ¡Que lejos estoy del suelo donde he nacido! Inmensa nostalgia invade mi pensamiento; y al ver me tan solo y triste cual hoja al viento, quisiera llorar, quisiera morir de sentimiento.
> ¡O tierra del sol! Suspiro por verte, ahora que lejos yo vivo sin luz, sin amor; y al verme tan solo y triste cual hoja al viento, quisiera llorar, quisiera morir de sentimiento.
> [How far I am from the land where I was born!
> An intense sadness invades my thought;
> I am so alone and sad, like a leaf shaking in the wind,
> I want to cry, I want to die from these feelings.
> Oh, land of the sun! I yearn to see you
> now that I live so far away—without your light, without love;
> I am so alone and sad, like a leaf shaking in the wind,
> I want to cry, I want to die from these feelings.][2]

"Canción mixteca" is ubiquitous in Oaxaca. It is sung at parties and performances throughout the state and by indigenous as well as mestizo Oaxacans. The song describes a pull exerted by the homeland that is so strong, a migrant will die of loneliness and heartache if he cannot return. Rather than describing a chase for money, the song tells of the hold that geography and, by extension, traditional culture has on migrants as they move.

The images created in these songs are powerful and profound, but they are also unrealistic. We should not assume that Velázquez described a nation's experiences in his song of the Norteños or that López Alvaréz was any more accurate about Oaxacans in his ode to the Mixtecos. Nevertheless, the images in these songs are powerful, and they do reference certain kinds of experiences that characterize at least some of the outcomes that migrants talk about.

The term "Norteño" describes a kind of migrant who originates in northern Mexico and is drawn to the United States by the combined pull

The band at a fiesta in San Juan del Estado, June 2000. Author photo.

of a labor market that promises wealth and the push of local economies that promise little. Caught between failed local systems and the seduction of the United States, the Norteño fills a middle world that transcends borders but at the same time lacks roots in either Mexico or the United States.

The image found in "Canción mixteca" contrasts with that of the Norteño. For Mixtecos, and for all rural Oaxacans by association, the ties to homeland are more than important; they are a force that centers the migrant and gives him hope even when he is away. Unlike Norteños, Mixtecos are not chasing dollars; rather they are looking homeward, with a nostalgia that keeps them connected.

I have a reason for bringing up these two images as a way to begin this study. Often in migration studies, the analysis focuses on a specific and singular cause of movement. A Norteño-like model describes migrants as laborers searching for relatively high wages. The story finds its counterpart in the push-pull models of the migration economists that date to early research on the subject by Ravenstein (1889).[3] In contrast, the essentialist framework provided in "Canción mixteca" suggests that tradition and geography are the critical determinative forces in a migrant's decision to leave.

The economist's model argues that the supply of underpaid labor in Mexico and the presence of higher wages in the United States drives migration between the two countries. Hometowns in Mexico lack infrastructure and opportunity, while in the United States, good-paying jobs go wanting. In response, rural Mexicans join the ranks of migrants entering the United States by the millions.

The successes of U.S.-bound migrants bring more individuals. The pool of potential migrants expands further as successful migrants return to hometowns with money and new ideas. Migration becomes a self-reinforcing process as more individuals join the flow of labor across the border, and so on (Massey 1990).

Nevertheless, people do not blindly follow migrants as they leave. A large percentage of any community remains "immobile" (at home) even as migration rates increase (see chapter 5). Thus, although a push-pull model based in labor market demand tells us something about one force behind migration, it cannot explain the variations encountered among migrants, their households, and their communities (see discussion in Massey et al. 1998, 45–50).

A model that argues that geography and tradition are critical forces in determining outcomes is no more satisfying (see critiques of essentialism by Mitchell 1995 and Watanabe 1992). To suggest that traditions, culture, and place drive people in their decision making maintains the fiction that we are at the mercy of superorganic forces beyond our control.

In such a system, migrants do not decide where they will go, what they will do, or how they will get where they are going. Instead, they respond to cultural influences and other forces that cannot be defined in economic or political terms. In other words, migrants follow certain patterns as they move, because they are rural, traditional folk, and that is what rural, traditional folk do.[4]

Of course, migrants are not cultural automatons. Traditions do not drive migrants to make certain decisions, nor do inequalities in the labor market always determine migrants' final destinations. Migrants are individuals, and they bring certain qualities—personal strengths and weaknesses—to their decisions that include education, experience, and expectations for the future. Migrants are also members of households. They are embedded in social networks that are rooted in kinship and friendship, that connect households locally and beyond, and that are maintained through cooperative and reciprocal ties (see Cohen 1999). Finally, they are also members of communities, which further influence outcomes. And although regional patterns in Oaxaca are apparent, communities are unique. Each community is geographically different, with its own specific history, economy, and ties to external forces. Thus migrants make their decisions in response not only to their individual strengths but also to the strengths of their households and communities (Faist 1997; Fischer et al. 1997; Hammar and Tamas 1997).

Some migrants choose to embrace their families and households—remitting to support the group. Some choose to leave and sever ties with their households and communities. Some Oaxacans take the role of the Norteño and are forever chasing a pot of dollars and the promise of economic success. Others migrate, but always with the goal of return. Some migrants succeed, whiles others fail and disappear.

Mutersbaugh (2002) argues that Oaxacan communities will exile migrants and set up serious sanctions for sojourners who have traveled for too many years. Nevertheless, the majority of central valley Oaxacans who do migrate (and a surprising number never leave their communities of origin) elect to travel for no more than about a year total, and throughout that time they send money home to support their families and by extension their community.

For the typical Oaxacan migrant the decision to move is not uncommon or exceptional, whether he or she elects to travel to a destination in Mexico or to the United States. Rather, migration in the central valleys is pervasive and commonplace. Moore (1988, 96) describes migration as "part of a strategy for coping with economic change, and opportunity which depends on multiplex links being established between rural and urban areas." It is part of everyday life and perhaps best understood in terms of what is a "culture of migration."

By "culture of migration," I mean to argue, first, that migration is pervasive—it occurs throughout the region and has a historical presence that dates to the first half of the twentieth century. Second, the decision to migrate is one that people make as part of their everyday experiences. Third and finally, the decision to migrate is accepted by most Oaxacans as one path toward economic well-being.

A culture of migration captures how I understand migration to work in Oaxaca. The choice comes from the interplay of individuals, their households, and their communities, as well as national and international socioeconomic forces. To call migration in Oaxaca "cultural" is not to say it is some kind of hard-wired response—or an automatic reaction to a set of specific outcomes. Instead, migration is one response among many to patterns and processes that link households and rural communities to global labor markets, flows of goods, and personal demands. In other words, migration in Oaxaca is "deeply ingrained into the repertoire of people's behavior, and values associated with migration become part of the community's values" (Massey et al. 1998, 47).

SOME BACKGROUND

Over the last six years, I have investigated migration patterns in twelve communities in rural Oaxaca, Mexico. Oaxaca is a poor state in the south of the country that faces serious economic, environmental, and social challenges. It is home to a large pool of migrants, and some days it seems as though every town has lost a substantial number of its able-bodied young men and women to the seductive pull of the United States. In towns like San Juan Guelavia, about 60% of the community's households have sent members to the United States, and on average about 40% of the households in central valley communities include U.S.-bound migrants.

Nevertheless, according to the Instituto Nacional de Estadísticas Geografía e Informática (INEGI), Oaxacan migration to the United States is a small percentage of the overall flow of migrants from Mexico to the United States. The state was ranked sixteenth of thirty-one Mexican states in terms of migration. Furthermore, INEGI estimated that movements of rural Oaxacans remained relatively low through the year 2000, given national patterns (INEGI 2002a, 2002b).[5]

INEGI found that 96.8% of the state's population of just over 3 million individuals above the age of five were in their natal hometowns in 1995. A relatively small group of Oaxacans (2.5%) was moving internally within the state, and 2.8% were moving either within Mexico or to another country. For those Oaxacans moving out of the state, 91.2% remained within Mexico's national border, and 8.8% (7,439 individuals) crossed into another country (INEGI 2002a, 2002b).[6]

To understand where Oaxaca fits—to make sense of why migration matters even if the state ranks rather low relative to other states—I focused on understanding the history of movement, the impact of migration, and the importance of migrant remittances (the moneys that migrants return to their families) for rural Oaxacans from the central valleys region. I began this work in 1996, with three goals in mind: to contextualize Oaxacan migration, to define the place of ethnicity in migration outcomes, and to develop a model that will explain Oaxacan migration in relation to broader national patterns.

Over the years, I have met Oaxacan migrants who were home to attend fiestas, to celebrate weddings, or to mourn at funerals. I watched as

Collecting an oral history, San Pedro Ixtlahuaca, July 2001. Author photo.

these migrants quickly left to return to the United States (*el otro lado,* the other side) to jobs, new families, and new challenges. I sat in plazas with native-born men and women who looked as out of place in their hometowns as any foreigner. I even met the occasional child born to migrant parents and sent home to Oaxaca for a summer with grandparents. Some of these children spoke very little Spanish (communicating instead in English), had never lived in a rural setting, and had little sense of or interest in peasant life in Oaxaca.

However, I met few migrants who behaved like Norteños. In general, the men and women I encountered over the years were fathers and mothers with small children whom they had to leave behind in Oaxaca. These migrants boarded buses in Oaxaca City's second-class bus station, with tears streaming down their faces. Clutching small bags with a few changes of clothes and the telephone number and address of a relative, they began their trek north, seeking jobs in the United States. These were not solitary migrants hiding in the shadows; rather they were mothers and fathers, brothers and sisters, sons and daughters, struggling to balance the demands of their families against their own wishes for the future.

Oaxacan migrants work hard to balance their temporary sojourns to other parts of Mexico and the United States with the demands of family, home, and community. They make their trips to the United States as members of resilient social networks that develop from ties of kinship and friendship. In fact, few migrants travel to the United States without a destination in mind and a friend or relative to meet (see chapter 3).

The migrants I know are deeply committed to their families. They migrate to support children, siblings, and parents. They risk their health and their lives for the good of their families and households. Usually they do not leave for long. Instead, they return to their hometowns after a year or two (sometimes three) to farm, to serve in local government, and to regain or perhaps renew their self-image as valuable, honest, and hardworking citizens of their communities.

With so much migration in the news and with such an emphasis in anthropology on the study of migration, it is easy to forget that many Oaxacans never leave their hometowns. Over the years, I have encountered many nonmigrants, people who have not and will not migrate for one reason or another (see chapter 5). So yes, I find the typical, dislocated migrant, but more often I meet *gente humilde* (humble folk)—fathers, mothers, sons, and daughters who face a changing world with grace and dignity as they manage the need for migration against other demands in an effort to maintain family, home, and community.

In this book, I introduce you to rural Oaxacans from communities in the state's central valleys. I let these people tell you about their experiences in their own words. First, I want to introduce you to the state and to describe some of the theoretical models that are used in the study of migration, including the household model I have developed. I also share with you why I believe anthropology is well positioned to interpret migration outcomes and remittance use.

THE CENTRAL VALLEYS OF OAXACA, MEXICO

Oaxaca is a unique place. Along with Chiapas, Oaxaca is one of Mexico's most ethnically diverse states. One reason I chose to do this work in Oaxaca was to discover whether there were differences between the migration experiences of indigenous and mestizo (nonindigenous) Mexicans. The communities that make my sample include Zapotec, Chinantec, and mestizo villages.

Rural Oaxaca. Author photo.

Given Oaxaca's status as one of Mexico's most "indigenous" places, it should come as little surprise that it is a poor, rural state. Oaxaca holds a distinctive spot at the bottom of most economic indicators such as per capita income, industrialization, and employment. The infrastructures of most rural communities are fragmentary at best, and basic services like running water, sewerage, and phone service remain difficult to find outside the state's capital. Oaxaca also ranks poorly in terms of health and social status indicators, with a high infant mortality rate and a low literacy rate, for example. Nevertheless, Oaxaca is not an isolated place. It is not a timeless world where Indians follow ancient rituals and calendars. Rather Oaxaca is part of the growing global capitalist system linked through tourism, development, education, entertainment, and migration.

The central valleys comprise the intermontane region that surrounds Oaxaca City (the state's capital) and includes the Centro, Etla, Ocotlán, Tlacolula, and Zimatlán districts. Communities in the central valleys are relatively well off when compared with those in the rest of the state. In general, communities in the central valleys are linked to Oaxaca City through bus and taxi service. The local economies of these communities are tied to the city, which attracts thousands of day laborers (accounting for

TABLE 0.1 COMMUNITIES SURVEYED

Community	*District*	*Distance from Oaxaca City (km)*	*Population (in 2000)*	*Households surveyed*	*Migrant households*
San Pablo Huitzo	Etla	31	5,066	41	9
San Juan del Estado		27	2,277	66	35
Guadalupe Etla		19	2,000	66	30
San Pedro Ixtlahuaca	Centro	10	3,599	50	26
Santa María Guelacé	Tlacolula	23	753	28	12
San Juan Guelavia		37	2,919	87	54
Villa Díaz Ordaz		40	5,583	61	25
San Lorenzo Albarradas		68	2,542	56	17
San Juan del Río		85	1,349	47	20
Santa Ana del Valle		35	2,140	54	34
Santa Inés Yatzeche	Zimatlán	40	1,175	30	17
San Martín Tilcajete	Ocotlán	23	2,776	58	30

at least 10% of the city's workforce—INEGI 1999). The city offers opportunities for education and is an important tourist destination for foreign travels.

I chose to work in the central valleys for several reasons. First, I am most familiar with the central valleys region of the state—particularly the eastern arm of the valley where Santa Ana del Valle is situated (see Cohen 1999). Second, the presence of mestizo and indigenous communities in the valley meant that I could examine the role of ethnicity in migration outcomes. Third, the differences that separate central valley communities are not so great as to make their comparison difficult.[7]

In general, these are rural villages where small-scale agricultural production is found alongside craft production and limited wage labor. Communities from more isolated regions of the state are much different and lack access to the city and its opportunities (see Kearney 2000).

I chose eleven central valley communities for this study from a randomized list that Dr. Martha Rees of Agnes Scott College created for the central valleys region (see table 0.1 and map). The communities are located in one of the three branches of Oaxaca's central valleys (the Etla, Tlacolula, and Ocotlán/Zimatlán valleys) with the exception of San Pedro Ixtlahuaca, which is in the Centro district, 10 kilometers west of Oaxaca City.

The Etla valley extends from Oaxaca City on an axis from west to northwest and includes the communities of San Pablo Huitzo (31 km from the capital), San Juan del Estado (27 km), and Guadalupe Etla (19 km). South of the city the communities of San Martín Tilcajete (23 km) and Santa Inés Yatzeche (40 km) are in the Ocotlán/Zimatlán valleys. Finally, to the east and in the Tlacolula valley are Santa María Guelacé (23 km), San Juan Guelavia (37 km), Santa Ana del Valle (34 km), Villa Díaz Ordaz (40 km), San Lorenzo Albarradas (68 km), and San Juan del Río (80 km).

From afar, these dozen communities look very much alike. Brick, adobe, and cement-block homes of one or two stories with red tile roofs fill villages that radiate in standard block grids from the central plaza. The plazas are constructed around central churches, governmental buildings, and small market areas. Often the plaza includes at least one basketball court where competitions are held nightly, a band shelter, and other public spaces. Circling the communities are dusty farmlands that look tired and overused to the untrained eye. Nevertheless, land in the central valleys is fertile, and households in our survey produced enough maize to support themselves for six months to one year from nonirrigated fields (described as *temporal,* or rain-fed, lands) that averaged about 1 hectare in size.

Central valley communities share many demographic and socioeconomic attributes. These communities have experienced dramatic increases in population since the 1950s. The total population for the twelve communities in our data set grew from 19,254 in the 1950 census to 33,261 in the year 2000 (INEGI 2002b; SEN 1953). The increase in population has come with a rise in the demand for wage labor, schooling, services (electricity, running water), and medical care. Unfortunately, the infrastructure of these communities remains underdeveloped, and the market for labor is limited. In other words, there are few opportunities for wage labor, few doctors, poor schools, and limited access to market goods—all important motivations for migration.

A review of work and wages in the state illustrates the challenges facing most Oaxacans. The Mexican government defines a living wage as two times the daily minimum. In Oaxaca, the daily minimum has hovered around US$5 for the decade of the 1990s. Surveys by INEGI note that on average 80% of the households in these communities make no more than twice the minimum—in other words a living wage (INEGI 2001a). For specific communities, the percentage of households making less than twice the minimum ranges from 55% and 59% in San Pablo Huitzo and Guada-

TABLE 0.2 MINIMUM WAGE RATES

Community	*% of population earning twice minimum wage or less*
Guadalupe Etla	59
San Juan del Estado	73
San Juan del Río	93
San Juan Guelavia	78
San Lorenzo Albarradas	90
San Martín Tilcajete	81
San Pablo Huitzo	55
San Pedro Ixtlahuaca	69
Santa Ana del Valle	91
Santa Inés Yatzeche	94
Santa María Guelacé	83
Villa Díaz Ordaz	92

Source: DIGEPO 1999.

lupe Etla, respectively, to 93% and 94% of the households in San Juan del Río and Santa Inés Yatzeche. In other words, in San Juan del Río and Santa Inés Yatzeche only 6 to 7% of local households make more than twice the minimum wage (table 0.2).

An average of 51% of the adults over the age of fifteen had not completed *primaria* (the first six years of primary school). Men had completed an average of about half a year more of school than women in the communities surveyed (on gender and education, see Kowalewski and Saindon 1992). Guadalupe Etla had the highest education rate, with 78% of its adults completing *primaria.* At the other extreme, 70% of the adults in Santa Inés Yatzeche had not completed the six years of compulsory education mandated by the government (table 0.3).

Educational opportunities are limited to primary school, although San Pablo Huitzo and San Pedro Ixtlahuaca are home to *telesecundarias* (closed-circuit high schools). Students interested in additional education must travel to nearby cities or the state capital. Health care is lacking throughout the state, and only 23% of the state's population have direct access to health care (INEGI 2002a, 2002b). Health care in the communities we surveyed included *casas de salud* (health clinics) that are part of the national health care system (Secretaría de Salubridad).

Infrastructure in the central valleys, including electrification, is problematic at best, and access to basic services like water and sewers continues to lag (table 0.4). Where improvements occur, they are largely self-funded or funded through a combination of local and state monies. To cover the costs of development, village leaders assess fees for households in their community. These funds, called *cooperación,* pay for projects and programs for which there is no, or only limited, state funding. *Cooperación* is one dimension of the traditional model of social organization and control that Oaxacans rely upon and that are found in most communities. The state describes this system as *usos y costumbres* (literally "uses and customs," but more accurately translated as "traditional practices"), and the system contrasts with the party politics of larger cities and Mexico in general (see Fox and Aranda 1996).

In addition to *cooperación,* traditional patterns of reciprocity, cooperation, and community participation are defined by *tequio* and by service in the *cargo* system. *Tequio* is communal labor organized by a community's leaders. Leaders can call for *tequio* at any time of the year to cover the labor needed for projects and programs in a village. *Tequio* depends upon households to contribute one worker each to projects that can range from the simple to the complex. Households typically send members to participate in *tequio* at least once a year, or they sometimes hire a replacement to cover

TABLE 0.3 ILLITERACY AND EDUCATION LEVELS

	Illiteracy rate (%)	*Adults who have not completed* primaria *(%)*
Guadalupe Etla	6	22
San Juan del Estado	13	45
San Juan del Río	25	60
San Juan Guelavia	21	52
San Lorenzo Albarradas	18	62
San Martín Tilcajete	11	40
San Pablo Huitzo	6	28
San Pedro Ixtlahuaca	14	40
Santa Ana del Valle	11	49
Santa Inés Yatzeche	46	70
Santa María Guelacé	10	37
Villa Díaz Ordaz	19	56

Source: DIGEPO 1999.

TABLE 0.4 ACCESS TO SERVICES

	% of households with		
Community	*No sewer*	*No electricity*	*No water service*
Guadalupe Etla	7	3	14
San Juan del Estado	7	5	3
San Juan del Río	4	1	—
San Juan Guelavia	25	1	98
San Lorenzo Albarradas	14	7	22
San Martín Tilcajete	18	2	23
San Pablo Huitzo	8	3	67
San Pedro Ixtlahuaca	31	6	43
Santa Ana del Valle	56	—	60
Santa Inés Yatzeche	16	6	12
Santa María Guelacé	6	1	1
Villa Díaz Ordaz	28	3	4

Source: DIGEPO 1999.

their commitments. Community leaders can impose sanctions on households that fail to support *tequio* or that fail to send members to serve in labor brigades.

The *cargo* system is at the heart of village politics in rural Oaxaca. *Cargos* are the burdens that members of households must endure to maintain their household's status in their community (Cancian 1965). The *cargo* system contrasts with politics that are administered *por partidos* (party based).[8] Households participate in the *cargo* system voluntarily. However, town leaders typically exert intense pressure upon household heads to send individuals to serve (see Cohen 1999). The response to noncompliant households includes sanctions that range from fines to expulsion.

Individuals volunteer or are nominated to positions in the system and serve terms of one to three years, depending on the nature of the *cargo*. In general, one adult member of any household in a community must serve in a committee every other year (although many exceptions are made to service). In the past, service was restricted to adult males. However, partly in response to the growing number of men who have migrated from their home communities, adult women are now serving in *cargos*.

The system of *cargos* includes a series of hierarchically arranged committees and positions that organize the political and civil life of the village.

Three key committees typically occupy the highest positions in the hierarchy: the *comite del pueblo, bienes comunales* (common lands), and the *comite del templo* (church committee). The *presidente municipal* (village president) chairs the *comite del pueblo* and manages a board that usually includes seven *suplentes* (board members), a *tesorero* (treasurer), a *síndico* (organizer), and *secretario* (secretary). *Bienes comunales* is the second high-ranking committee that manages a community's natural resources. Finally, the *comite del templo* manages the spiritual life of the village, caring for the village's church and saints and planning rituals throughout the year. Dozens of committees follow these in descending rank and status, ranging from school committees (like the PTA in North America) to committees concerned with transportation, roads, water, utilities, and so forth.

Even with the common patterns and practices noted above, there are important differences among the various communities. The most obvious difference divides communities in terms of their ethnic makeup. San Juan Guelavia, Santa Ana del Valle, Villa Díaz Ordaz, San Juan del Río (all in the Tlacolula branch of the valley), and Santa Inés Yatzeche are indigenous communities with populations that continue to speak Zapotec in the home.

A recent survey was conducted by the Dirección General de Población de Oaxaca y el Consejo Nacional de Población (DIGEPO) to examine rural marginality, as measured by literacy rates, access to running water, access to health care, and employment patterns. The survey discovered that indigenous communities (including all of the indigenous villages in the present study) were marked by extreme socioeconomic marginality. Mestizo communities ranked low as well, but none scored as poorly as did indigenous communities. This is one indication that ethnicity correlates with poverty in rural Mexico, and indigenous communities are at an increased disadvantage.[9]

Craft specialization is a second factor that divides these communities into different camps. San Juan Guelavia, Santa Ana del Valle, San Martín Tilcajete, San Lorenzo Albarradas, and Villa Díaz Ordaz are linked to the local craft market and the global tourist industry in profound ways, even though farming remains central to household survival.

San Martín Tilcajete is perhaps the best known of the craft-producing communities we surveyed. San Martín Tilcajete is the home of Alebrijes, brightly painted wooden animals and zoomorphic figures that are extremely popular tourist items (Chibnik 2001). The community is prosperous, and signs of the booming market for wood carvings are everywhere, from the refurbished village plaza that includes a covered basketball court

Weavers in Villa Díaz Ordaz, June 2001. Author photo.

to the numerous two- and three-story homes that are wired for satellite television. Wood carving involved 57% of the households we surveyed in San Martín Tilcajete. The income that households are able to earn from production and the sale of goods on the market is strong enough to slow out-migration.[10] One carver described the situation to us in a matter-of-fact fashion:

> I can earn plenty right here, and maybe in the U.S. I could earn ten times more, but it costs too much and there are too many risks. So why would I travel to California and spend 10,000 pesos, when I can stay right here?
> SALVADOR JIMENEZ, SAN MARTÍN TILCAJETE, JANUARY 2002[11]

Santa Ana del Valle and Villa Díaz Ordaz are in a different situation. Both communities participate in the production of woolen textiles for sale in local tourist markets and for export. However, unlike San Martín Tilcajete, these communities do not dominate production. Instead, the textile production in these towns follows a contract-labor model that the weavers described as *mano de obra* (piecework).

Buyers and intermediaries from the community of Teotitlán del Valle dominate the market and control prices, sales, and production (see Stephen 1991). In other words, craft producers from Santa Ana del Valle and Villa Díaz Ordaz do not control the production or sale of their goods. I found that 56% of Santa Ana del Valle's weavers work on contract with intermediaries from Teotitlán (Cohen 1999, 48). The percentage of artisan households in Villa Díaz Ordaz is much lower (13%). Households in Villa Díaz Ordaz lack access to the market, and problems with access likely limit production. Weavers in Santa Ana del Valle and Villa Díaz Ordaz do not earn enough from their work to make migration more of a choice and less of a necessity. In fact, weavers in both towns described craft production as little more than a means to an end.

San Juan Guelavia and San Lorenzo Albarradas also produce crafts, *canastas* (baskets) in the former and *petates* (reed mats) in the latter. However, these crafts are sold almost entirely on the local market. Except for the *petates* that tourists buy to use at the beach, the mat is an item that rural Oaxacans buy to use for a bed. San Juan Guelavia's baskets appeal to a local market as well. The townsfolk make baskets that are primarily used for hauling corn, groceries, and goods from one place to another. The baskets are not generally marketed to tourists, and they tend toward the utilitarian. Unfortunately, the market for handmade baskets has come under pressure from ready-made plastic containers and bags, and even though 38% of the households we surveyed produced *canastas,* no one earned a living wage from that work. Rather, basketmaking was something that Guelavians did outside of farm labor as a way to supplement income. The rising cost of supplies for the baskets is also a stress on business. Don Epiphanio Garcia described the situation for us:

> We used to be able to go to the river [Río Salado] and just take all of the cane [*caña*] we wanted. But it has disappeared. Now we have to go to Pochutla or somewhere else to buy cane, and it is expensive. A load costs a peso per stem! Many of us are giving up—there is no market, and it is just too much money to produce.
>
> EPIPHANIO GARCIA, SAN JUAN GUELAVIA, JUNE 2000

Basket maker, San Juan Guelavia, June 2000. Author photo.

San Lorenzo Albarradas has a second way of tapping into the tourist economy. The community is home to natural mineral springs called Hierve el Agua (the name literally means "boiling water"). Working with several nongovernmental organizations (NGOs), the town is involved in a series of programs to develop its natural resource.

Santa Inés Yatzeche and San Juan del Río are in much more precarious economic positions. Their local economies are defined by farming and little else. Neither town is home to a craft tradition, and the land in San Juan del Río in particular is of marginal quality for farming. It will come as no surprise that DIGEPO's survey found indicators of marginality high in both communities. Santa Inés Yatzeche benefits somewhat from its proximity to Zimatlán, and households can sell produce there. Nevertheless, few jobs are available in Zimatlán, and most of Santa Inés Yatzeche's populace must travel to Oaxaca City if they want to find local wage work.

Santa María Guelacé is also a town defined by farming, with no craft production present. However, unlike Santa Inés Yatzeche and San Juan del

Río, Santa María Guelacé has a good portion of irrigated land, and its proximity to Oaxaca City makes it much easier for its population to find work. The community is also home to *ajieros* (garlic producers), who sell their goods to restaurants in the city.

Urbanism is also an important marker of difference in the valleys. Guadalupe Etla, San Pablo Huitzo, San Juan del Estado, and San Pedro Ixtlahuaca are larger, urban centers with more dynamic local economies, and they stand apart from the rest of the communities surveyed for this study. San Pablo Huitzo serves as a minor market center for villages that surround it, as does San Juan del Estado. San Juan del Estado's lands support a small lumber industry and a stone quarry. Finally, Guadalupe Etla has become a bedroom community for urban Oaxacans who are looking for a suburban lifestyle.

San Pedro Ixtlahuaca is the closest to Oaxaca City of the towns we surveyed. Only 10 kilometers due west of Oaxaca, the community is tucked below the archaeological site of Monte Albán and has rich agricultural lands. Like Guadalupe Etla, San Pedro Ixtlahuaca is home to a growing community of urban Oaxacans who are leaving the city. In San Pedro Ixtlahuaca this change has led to some tensions as newcomers and established families struggle over the value and importance of traditional political practices.

There are differences in the migration rates for each community. These differences are discussed in detail in chapter 1, but here it is important to understand, first, that migration is not uniform across the communities and, second, that it is not homogeneous across a community's households. Migration in rural Oaxaca on average involves about 47% of a community's households, but there is a great deal of variation from one community to the next. Similarly, each community has households that cannot or will not migrate.

UNDERSTANDING MEXICAN MIGRATION

"Migration" is a term that social scientists use to define and describe movement by human populations. Migration does not occur in a vacuum. People do not migrate because they must. We are not animals that have some deep-seated need to complete a circuit in response to some biological drive. Rather, humans migrate because they can. People make decisions to migrate in response to desires, lifestyles, resources, and needs.

To get an idea of where Oaxacan migration and Mexican migration in general fit into this process, let me review some basic facts about Mexican-U.S. migration. Millions of Mexicans live legally and illegally in the United States. Van Hook and Bean (1998) estimate that just over 7 million Mexicans live in the United States and that 2.35 million of those Mexicans were in the United States without authorization (see also Lozano Ascencio 1998, 1209). Oaxacans are a small group within this larger population. INEGI (2001b) estimates that Oaxacans account for no more than about 4% of the total migrant population currently in the United States—or nearly 100,000 individuals. In contrast, nearly 70% of Mexico's migrants come from just ten states: Michoacán, Guanajuato, and Jalisco (three traditional sending regions), along with Zacatecas, Durango, Mexico City, Chihuahua, Tamaulipas, Guerrero, and the state of Mexico (Bustamante et al. 1998, 116). There has been little overall change in the makeup of this population over the last thirty years, according to Marcelli and Cornelius (2001). Readers might ask, why should we be so concerned with Oaxacan migrants in the United States? The answer comes in at least two parts.

First, even though Oaxacans account for a small percentage of the total migrant population living in the United States, the economic effects of their moves are profound for Oaxaca, amounting to at least US$11 million returned to the state during the 1990s alone (Lozano Ascencio 1993). Second, there are positive and negative social costs of movement, and the debate continues over just what migration means for rural Mexicans in general. The history and outcomes of migration for rural Oaxacans from the state's central valleys offer an important comparison to better-known sending regions.

MIGRATION AND REMITTANCES

Migration is not just about moving across the landscape. Migration is also about sending money home, or remitting. A second theme of this book focuses on what remittances mean for rural Oaxacans, and the positive and negative impacts that remittances can have on rural society. Mexican migrants (including migrants from Oaxaca) remit as much as US$3 billion annually to families in Mexico (Lozano Ascencio 1998, 1192), an amount that equals or exceeds the income generated by agricultural exports and tourism (see Lozano Ascencio 1993, 64, figure 5; Russell 1992; Taylor et al. 1996b).[12]

Remittances can be used to positive ends (see Orozco 2002). Richard Jones (1998, 4) notes that remittances in Mexico are "safety nets for poor regions left behind by the agglomerative behavior of international capital, by the preoccupation of the international community with other matters, and by the indifference of their own government" (see also Bustamante et al. 1998 and Taylor 1999). However, migration is more than a process that leads to economic change for rural communities. It is also a process that has social and cultural costs and benefits that individuals initiate as members of households and communities. Thus it is probably not surprising that the debate continues over how best to explain outcomes of migration and the use of remittances for rural peasant households and their communities.

Although social scientists use many models to explore migration (see, for example, Brettell and Hollifield 2000), two competing ideas—development and dependency—dominate much of the debate. Those who favor dependency models focus on the socioeconomic costs of migration, whereas proponents of development models point toward the economic growth that comes from remittance use. Dependency models argue that migration exacerbates local socioeconomic inequalities and drives unproductive consumption within migrant households while creating pools of cheap labor waiting to be exploited (Reichert 1981). The result is a place where the population, in its quest to find the money necessary to purchase the goods it now wants, becomes addicted to migration. A population directs its energies not toward internal balance and progress but toward external markets, because the community lacks any kind of infrastructure that can support local labor and the creation of local market outlets. In other words, rural communities are dependent on distant centers of power for jobs and goods. Rural communities caught in this kind of a web become little more than nurseries for the young (future migrants) and "homes" for the elderly (those no longer able to migrate). The outcome of this process is the social disintegration of sending communities: the able-bodied residents are siphoned away by the pull of job opportunities and the disruption of local practices, as remittances are wasted (see Brana-Shute and Brana-Shute 1982; Diaz Briquets 1991; Guidi 1993; Martin 1991; Papademetriou 1991; and Rubenstein 1992).

Researchers who argue for development models emphasize the benefits of migration and the potential positive outcomes as remittances flow back to rural hometowns where there are few opportunities and even fewer wage-based jobs (Taylor 1999, 73). There is strong evidence that "migradollars" (the dollars generated through transnational migration) can foster economic growth nationally and locally (Durand et al. 1996a, 1996b; Smith 1998; Taylor et al. 1996a, 1996b).

Remittances are critical to national economies, and they are an important source of foreign exchange. The funds sent home by Mexicans living and working in the United States become the hard currency that the Mexican state needs to balance its deficits (Massey et al. 1998, 232). These funds also drive the expansion of the national economy; as a 1990 report indicated, "each migradollar entering Mexico ultimately produced a $2.90 increase in Mexico's Gross Domestic Product and raised output by a total of $3.20" (Durand et al. 1996a).

Nevertheless, these are national outcomes. At a local level, the impact of remittances is more varied. The majority of the remittances that are returned to central valley households go to covering the costs of household maintenance (see de la Garza and Orozco 2002, 37). Investments and savings, though they do occur, come only after households meet their basic expenses. This means that although remittances can become the basis for what informants describe as the self-advancement of their households, families, and villages, in general they do not. When remittances are invested, they underwrite the expansion of services, such as water and electricity, and the support and revival of community rituals. The money returned also helps families cover the costs of participating in the political life of their village (see Orozco 2002 and Smith 1998).

Remittances also carry costs for households and communities. Remittances can increase social inequalities that are rooted in local socioeconomic differences. As some households choose to migrate, others will not or cannot migrate. The result is that wealthy households that can afford migration's costs grow wealthier as they succeed. Households that cannot afford migration's costs are relatively impoverished in response. Furthermore, remittances will tend to decline over time and as migrants are away from their homes longer. Lowell and de la Garza (2002, 20) note that although 60% of all temporary Mexican migrants in the United States remit, the total dollars returned decline as migrants age and as the total number of years spent away from home increases.

A HOUSEHOLD MODEL OF MIGRATION

To understand migration decisions and the use of remittances in Oaxaca, I use a three-part, household-based approach.[13] This approach contrasts with macroeconomic models that focus on regional or sometimes national patterns in an effort to understand broadly based patterns of movement. A household model also contrasts with psychological models that focus on the migrant and explore migration and remittance outcomes from the perspective of the individual actor. Although both approaches have their strengths (macroeconomic models help us understand global patterns of movement, for example, while psychological models help us to define what qualities make for a successful migrant), neither model adequately addresses the social universe that defines migration for rural Oaxacans. An emphasis on the individual also causes trouble in the analysis of Oaxacan movement and misrepresents the ways in which households and communities inform how migrants define their social world.

To ignore the important role of the household is to misunderstand how rural Oaxacans create their social universe. The point is not to suggest that individuals are not decision makers, nor is it to argue that all migrants make their decisions in consultation with their household or in deference to communal concerns. In fact, in each community I have visited there are examples of individuals who turn their backs on families and communities and sever ties with their hometowns against the will of their parents and spouses. There are also examples of entire families or households who have left their communities. Nevertheless, the outcomes for the migrants who decide to sever ties and ignore their household's wishes are serious for those members of the household who are left behind. A household approach helps us capture this process and gain a better understanding of variation in outcomes. Finally, a household model reminds us that migration is not solely a process that pulls individuals to new labor markets so that they can improve incomes in relation to some abstract, distant social standard. Rather, as Massey et al. argue (1993, 438), migrants wish "to increase income relative to other households, and hence, to reduce their relative deprivation compared with some [well known and local] reference group."

METHODOLOGY

My approach, which defines migration as a decision rooted in the household and seeks to describe and predict patterns and outcomes for a region, has important ramifications for fieldwork and analysis. First, as pointed out above, it means we are not concerned so much with individual variation as with how that variation is rooted in the overall survival and status of the household or domestic group. Second, because we are interested in explaining variation, we must consider more than a single community's experiences. A focus on one community or population would make it difficult to define variation and to discover the various factors that influence and predict outcomes across space and time.

Therefore this study began by randomly selecting eleven communities from throughout the central valleys (with Santa Ana as a twelfth site). Because I was working in so many communities and because it was crucial to define large samples in each community, I could not do this work independently, in the traditional anthropological manner of the lone ethnographer. Instead I used a team of fieldworkers whom I helped train and who were coordinated through the Instituto Tecnológico de Oaxaca. Team-based research was a challenge for me, but it became an effective model that allowed for the definition of a large data set supporting both ethnographic and statistical analysis of migration outcomes.

Once I had selected communities for the project (with the help of a randomized list created by Martha Rees), the team began work in earnest. Over two summers we collected surveys in a randomly selected sample of 590 households, or about 15% of the households in each community. A household approach meant that we collected data on all the members of the domestic unit. In rural Oaxaca, the household could be difficult to define. In general, most rural households (63%) were nuclear units living in independent compounds, quite like their U.S. counterparts. In other words, the household included members of two generations living in a single homestead and pooling the resources and skills of its members. The senior generation consisted of a legally married couple; the junior generation included the offspring of the seniors. However, some households in the central valleys included more than two generations and were better thought of as extended units (35%). Typically, we found extended units organized around a married couple and their children, with the addition of a grandparent. Sometimes a household appeared to be an extended unit but was in fact a series of independent nuclear units that shared a common area or patio. Finally, some households defied classification (2%) and included odd mixtures of members. One memorable "other" was a household in San Juan del Estado that included three brothers in their late sixties. These brothers made their living by selling *carbon* (charcoal) and doing limited farmwork. They had no relatives in the community and in many ways existed as hermits.

We used maps from INEGI and plotted locations of potential households in each block within a community, ignoring blocks with no homes. We rotated the selection of households, moving from the northwest to the southwest, southeast, and northeast corners of consecutive blocks. Once we identified a location, a fieldworker received his or her map and began in the northwest corner, selected the first household counterclockwise from that corner, and knocked on the door to ask if he or she could conduct a survey, explaining our project and why it was important.[14] If members of a household refused to participate, the fieldworker proceeded to the next available house, going in a clockwise direction, and began the process again. In the event that no households in a block participated, the fieldworker moved to one in a series of "safe blocks" that were set aside for just this problem.

The survey included several sections and identified members of the domestic group, as well as their work, migration experience, land use, household organization, consumption patterns, and community participation. The first sections of the survey focused on household membership and organization (part 1), work (part 2), and migration experience (part 3). We assigned each household a unique code and described its members according to age, gender, civil status, place of birth and current residence, languages spoken, and education. We recorded work histories for all members involved in household maintenance, with attention to nonwage and informal labor (particularly among women) that is typically central and crucial to the domestic group's survival. We asked individuals to recount as many labor activities as they could remember and to identify how they combined various activities (farming and wage labor, for example) to meet the needs of the domestic group.

We identified migrants as we created inventories of a household's members and their activities in parts 1 and 2. Part 3 of the survey focused specifically on international and transnational (that is, back and forth) migration. In this section of the survey, we endeavored to gain a clear count of the total number of migrants in a household, as well as the number of trips members had taken. This was typically where we identified individuals who left their households and who no longer actively participated as members.[15] Migrants described their experiences, and we asked them to note their destinations; with whom they traveled; how they organized money to cover the expenses of border crossing; their work in the United States; with whom they stayed once they were settled; and their remittance history.

Next, in parts 4, 5, and 6, we asked about agriculture, household expenses, and housing. We created an inventory that included animals, goods and appliances, construction materials, and access to water and utilities (parts 4 and 5). We asked about weekly expenses for food, utilities, transportation, education, entertainment, and health care and how members covered those expenses (part 6). The last part of the survey focused on household members' participation in the social life of their village (part 7). We noted their political service, their participation and sponsorship of local rituals, and the reciprocal relationships they held with other families. Finally, we asked about their investment of time, money, and effort in village projects and programs.

We elicited detailed, personal responses on local social life, migration, and the structure of community by using open-ended questions built into the survey. After completing the surveys, we conducted follow-up interviews with community leaders and key informants to further document unique experiences. We also collected oral histories in each community. Fieldworkers identified informants for extended interviews and oral histories. In the final observation section of the survey, we noted if interviewees were "good talkers" and interested in sharing more of their experiences with us. We combined the surveys, interviews, oral histories, and additional archival work in Oaxaca City to create an ethnographically rich and dynamic picture of migration in the central valleys and to help illustrate how migration emerges from and interacts with local socioeconomic processes.

A second implication of a household approach is that it allows me to define migration as a stage-specific and predictable process that is influenced by the structure of the household (its members, their ages, their resources), local practices (sociocultural norms), regional economic trends, and macroeconomic forces. If migration follows specific stages, it means that outcomes are patterned and identifiable over time. In the case of Oaxacans from the central valleys, migration has peaked with each of Mexico's economic crises, and overall, sojourns to the United States have dramatically increased over the last two decades (see chapter 1).

The resources that are available to a household and its members can greatly influence the decision to migrate. Beyond the household, a community and its leadership also have some bearing on migration decisions and remittance use. Rural Oaxacan households maintain their status and standing in their communities through participation in a series of community-defined activities that include *tequio, servicio,* and *cooperación.* Households must also respect the demands that a community's leaders place on the population—the demand for participation in leadership, the demand for funds to support development projects, the demand that a migrant return home annually to avoid expulsion of his or her family (see Mutersbaugh 2002).

In addition to a community's resource base, access to regional markets, education, entertainment, and—perhaps most important—jobs has a great effect on migration outcomes and possibilities. Some of this effect is intuitive. Access to jobs in the state's capital, Oaxaca City, means there are local opportunities that Oaxacans living in isolated mountain communities lack. But resources also mean land and ways in which land can be used, and one point that will become clear is that a household's resource base is sometimes so strong as to make migration irrelevant—or, alternatively, the lack of resources can put migration out of reach for poorer households.

Regional demand for labor works both with and against international demand. The pull of jobs in the United States is a strong motivating force for Oaxacans seeking the money they need to feed their families, to buy consumer and luxury goods, and perhaps to start a new business. Through the early 1980s the seductive pull of higher wages came largely from Mexico City and other boomtowns within the nation. Now that pull is largely from the United States; nevertheless, the promise of wages is not in and of itself a force that will build migration. Rather, migrants and potential migrants also think about the dangers of the border and their reception once they have arrived. For some rural Oaxacans, fear of the border is more than enough to limit their desire to migrate, no matter the promise of wealth.

The third and last part of my approach defines the decisions to migrate and to use remittances as progressive (that is, made with the goal of satisfying the needs of the household), even though the outcomes of migration and remittances remain hard to predict. In other words, the decision to migrate is based in the experiences and strengths of the decision maker who "classifies the various alternatives in his [or her] subjective environment as to their expected outcomes, whether satisfactory or unsatisfactory" (Wolpert 1964, 544). Thus the migrant is an active agent who calculates within his or her abilities how to respond to opportunities and challenges. Migration becomes an option, not a given, and it is certainly not a process entered into blithely and with little prior knowledge.

These three points of investigation (the household, the stages of migration, and the progressive nature of decision making) resolve some of the contradictions that dependency and development models create. First, they allow us to move beyond the kinds of moralistic arguments that tend to dominate much of the debate on migration. The question of whether migration is good or bad is left behind, and we can instead focus on the patterns (whether local, regional, or global) that define and predict migration and remittance use outcomes. Second, the household model allows us to place individuals into their social milieu in a way that builds upon ethnographic analysis. Finally, because we define migrants as largely rational, we can better understand how they organize their resources and strategize to succeed.

STRUCTURE OF THE BOOK

Chapter 1 introduces the rural Oaxacan household and details why it is important to understand migration as part of a household's overall strategy for survival. Chapter 2 begins with a discussion of the history and geography of Oaxaca and the central valleys region. The history of movement for the area is reviewed to reinforce the point that although migration has increased rapidly over the last two decades, it is not a new process. I also review how Oaxacan migration to the United States links with local circuit moves (commutes from central valley communities to Oaxaca City) and movements within Mexico. Finally, the chapter details many of the factors that specialists believe are important predictors of migration. This list becomes important in chapter 3, where contemporary migration in the central valleys is discussed.

Chapter 3 focuses on contemporary migration outcomes. I share some of the false starts that plagued my team as we tried to understand the data we collected. The discussion also shows how we developed working models that bridge ethnographic and quantitative data to explain the outcomes of migration in the central valleys. I begin with a discussion of migration in general and why it is hard to aggregate the data. Three sections follow that focus on various kinds of moves, with examples from specific communities. My goal is not only to describe Oaxacan migration in detail but also to point out why we cannot focus solely on migration to the United States if we hope to understand local patterns of movement.

Chapter 4 examines the socioeconomic and cultural outcomes of migration and remittance use and the costs and benefits of movement. I focus on three areas: the revival of traditional celebrations that are paid for by remittances from migrants; the continued importance of traditional practices for the organization and maintenance of central valley communities; and strains that migration places on local communities.

Chapter 5 describes rural Oaxacans who do not migrate. One group of households does not migrate because the costs and risks are just too high and too great to make migration an option. The second group of households does not migrate because they are effectively able to maintain their households and cover any other kinds of expenses in a way that makes migration pointless. Land-poor, socially isolated households in San Juan del Estado illustrate those rural Oaxacans who cannot afford the risks of migrating. Dairy producers in Guadalupe Etla and craftspeople in San Martín Tilcajete illustrate the other extreme—Oaxacans who do not need to migrate, because they are doing well.

The conclusion returns to the question of how best to study migration and anthropology's role in migration studies. I argue that a household approach focused on domestic groups and their organization over time allows for a powerful analysis of migration and remittance use outcomes by articulating micro (ethnographic and detailed) data with macro (more generalized) data and models of migration outcomes (Brettell 2000). A second goal is to answer the question of whether a "culture of migration" exists in the central valleys. The evidence presented indicates that Oaxacan migration is embedded in a series of sociocultural patterns. Rather than destabilizing or undermining local cultural patterns and social processes, the decision to migrate can often support and even sometimes invigorate those patterns and processes. The outcome, then, is a culture of migration, a system in which migration is integrated and integral to ongoing sociocultural development.

Oaxacan migration is also embedded in global socioeconomic processes that include migration, tourism, education, market expansion, entertainment, health care, and so forth. There is no reason to think about Oaxaca as isolated—or as a home to native peoples who cannot cope with a changing world. The example of rural Oaxacans and their responses to global capitalism shows that there are better ways to describe natives and rural peoples. Studying the ways in which they respond to globalization accomplishes two important goals. First, it shows us that they are not victims of modernity but rather are people responding to the world and its inequalities in the best way they can. Second, the analysis continues to push anthropology beyond its romantic roots and toward a future where it can matter as a field.

One THE HOUSEHOLD AND MIGRATION

All my life I have farmed [a 1.5-hectare plot of irrigated land], and that land provides well for us. We harvested nearly eighteen months' worth of maize last year [1999]. But that wasn't enough. My family needed more help. I have three young children in school, and my two eldest sons [eighteen and twenty-one years of age]—they helped me in the field, but it wasn't enough. I sent them to the United States; that was a dangerous trip. But they went. I borrowed the money from friends to send them. They are there now; they live in Santa Monica, California. They are helping us out from there, paying for school and for the house.

DON CRISTOFORO MARTINEZ, SAN JUAN DEL ESTADO, MAY 2000

We have a son, José Luís, and he is working in Mexico [City]. Rosalva [daughter], she goes every day to work in a small shop in Oaxaca. Gilberto [son] works with me [the male household head] in the fields. That is the most important—farming [about 1 hectare of nonirrigated land]. José Luís, he left about five years ago. He lives with a cousin and works in construction. Sometimes he sends money home; sometimes he doesn't. He has his own family to worry about there. Rosalva lives here and travels daily on the bus to Oaxaca for work. Gilberto helps me—together we manage. I use some of Rosalva's money to buy seed. We [Doña Gloria does most of the selling] sell garlic and some other vegetables in the city and in the market.

MARTÍN GUTIERREZ AND GLORIA GARCÍA, SANTA MARÍA GUELACÉ, JUNE 2000

My husband went to the United States two years ago. He lives there with his brother in an apartment, I guess. I'm not sure where he is. He sends home about US$200 every other month for me and the children, sometimes less, sometimes more. We use that money for our home. I also use it to buy feed for my animals. The most important thing we do is to raise pigs for sale at Tlacolula or here. I can make between 1,600 and 2000 pesos for each pig—just last month we sold three pigs.

DOÑA AMELIA CAMARENA, SAN JUAN GUELAVIA, JULY 2001

To understand the importance and meaning of migration for rural Oaxacans, we cannot begin on the Mexican-U.S. border. Migration is not about arriving in Southern California, and as I argued in the introduction, it is not about migrants who live in some in-between world, with one foot in Mexico and the other firmly entrenched in the United States. Oaxacan migration begins in the decisions made by members of rural households. The decision to migrate takes account of that household's resources, the abilities of its members (both migrant and nonmigrant), the traditions of the community (including the history of migration), and the opportunities that the migrant's planned destination holds (see Kearney 1996). When I argue that migration is a decision made by a household, some questions will likely come to mind: What about migrants who sever their connections with their households and hometowns? What does it mean to say that the decision to migrate is made by a household and not by an individual?

The first question concerns migrants who sever at least some of their connections with their households and hometowns. Two distinct groups of migrants are of concern: migrants who leave, never to return and no longer in contact with their households; and migrants who remain in touch with their households in a limited sense but do not remit. The latter group includes migrants who sever some of the ties to their families but who do not necessarily abandon them fully. They may call home regularly and they might even visit, but they do not invest much of time or energy in the support of their family and hometown.

Although these migrants are not involved in the day-to-day maintenance of their former households, they can be important resources in receiving communities in the United States or elsewhere in Mexico. They serve as contacts and anchors for new immigrants who lack resources and experiences.

Migrants who ignore their households and communities sometimes reappear; at other times they may remit money in an unscheduled or unplanned way. Thus it is important to remember that social behavior is hard to predict, and today's missing migrant may become tomorrow's community supporter.

It is difficult to determine the number of migrants who fully disengage from their household upon leaving their hometowns. When I was in rural communities, talking to citizens about migration, I typically received one of two responses to the question, how many migrants are present here? Often a respondent would wave his or her hand in reference to the empty homes surrounding us and exclaim, "Everyone here has left. There are no adults here, only children and the elderly. All of the men are gone." The silence that greeted my team and me as we knocked on the doors of empty homes only reinforced the sense that everyone must be living in the United States. However, nearly as frequently, an informant would respond, "There are no migrants here"; and it was easy to underestimate migration when looking around a neighborhood bustling with energy and full of children and adults working together. Thus it can be hard to get a handle on migration rates—and for this reason we surveyed a random sample of households that were scattered throughout a community.

By collecting a random sample of households, we could better estimate migration rates. Nevertheless, what can we say about "missing" migrants? This was a tough issue to resolve. We used questions in our survey to try to determine the number and percentage of migrants who had left their households and severed all ties with their communities. When household heads talked about their migrant spouses, parents, and children, we asked where each migrant was, how much each migrant remitted, where that migrant was located, how the migrant covered the costs of movement, and where they were living at the time of the survey. We were able to ask these questions a couple of different ways (see appendix B). Informants described work and migration, and we asked for details on the household's members and their status (age, education, civil status, work, and community participation). By combining and cross-checking responses, we identified migrants, their locations, and whether they had severed ties with their families.

Relying on these cross-checks allowed us to better determine whether a migrant had disengaged from his or her household. We found that just fewer than 10% of the migrant households we surveyed described their homes as including migrants who were missing or uninvolved in the daily affairs of the domestic group. In other words, of the 256 households that included migrants as members, 25 described those migrants as having severed most if not all ties.[1] Additionally, another 15% of the migrant households we interviewed did not comment on the status of their migrating members.

The Díaz family, like the majority of migrant households, organized the money necessary to send its sons to the United States by turning to friends and relatives for support. The family sent two sons to Los Angeles. from their hometown of Santa Inés Yatzeche in early 2001. When we interviewed the household's heads in the summer of 2001, they commented, "Our sons are in Los Angeles, but they only just went, and we have not yet received anything from them." The Diazes anticipate that their sons will soon begin to remit—partly in response to the goodwill that sent them to the United States and partly to support their parents and siblings left behind. Nevertheless, how and when that would happen remained unresolved at the time of our interview.

Other households described losing their remittances when a son or daughter living in another part of Mexico or the United States married and established a family. In effect, the sending household—or the household of orientation that sent the migrant—was replaced by a new household formed around the migrant in his or her destination community (see Lowell and de la Garza 2002). There were also households that included migrants who remitted haphazardly. They might send a small amount of cash home every six months or at various times during the year. Sending households in such situations were forced to cover their own expenses and could not count upon regular remittances.

A household is fundamentally changed when an individual chooses to leave his or her family, when that individual does not remit funds to the household, and when the remaining members of the household talk about their lost and disappeared children, siblings, and (to a lesser degree) parents as if they were dead. In effect, the household that has lost a member or members has suffered a costly loss. It has lost potential supporters, important social connections, and the very people that ensure its continued health and well-being. The household that has lost members finds that its networks are limited and its future is less secure.

A new set of decisions faces the household that has lost members to migration.[2] How will the household survive as a unit? How will the household replace the labor of its missing member or members? Who will serve in the local civic hierarchy (the *cargo* system) if able-bodied adult men and women are no longer present? Perhaps the ultimate concern facing the household is who will serve as parents if children are left behind. Thus, rather than

A typical rural family with their anthropologist. Author photo.

discussing why a migrant leaves, I focus here on the organization of the migrant household.

Three areas are crucial to understanding household decision making with regard to migration, destinations, and remittance use over time. First, it is important to know a household's membership, its organization and gender makeup, and its stage in the development cycle (Fortes 1971; Netting et al. 1984). Second, we need to understand the social networks that are present and that migrants and potential migrants will use to support their moves over space and time. These networks also are critical in the organization and definition of household status within a community (Conway 2000; Massey 1990). Third and finally, we need to be aware of the unique social processes and cultural traditions of the households and communities we are studying and how those processes and traditions influence decision making and migration (Kearney 1995; Mines and Massey 1985; Wiest 1973).

A few examples from the central valleys illustrate the ways in which households organize for migration and how status and community and regional social patterns can define those outcomes. As I have pointed out, the loss of a member can be devastating to a household. Therefore it is important to remember that the decisions to migrate and to use remittances are made by households, but outcomes are still determined by the actions of individuals. To ignore the motivations that push an individual to migrate, even as we focus on the household decision making, risks overlooking just how delicate the balance is that exists between the individual and his or her domestic group. Even in our short interviews, this tension is apparent, as is clear from an interview with a young woman in Villa Díaz Ordaz. She had recently returned from a two-year trip to the United States. There she had worked as a maid for several hotels and lived with friends from her hometown community. She described the pressure that her parents placed on her as she struggled to keep up with a demanding work schedule that left little time for leisure.

> My parents sent me to live with my cousins, who found me my job. . . . I worked very hard and sent home everything I could. I just got too tired, and I didn't like it. It was crowded and noisy. I didn't want to stay, but I worked hard. I worked all day. I cleaned the rooms, made the beds. . . . I would come home and just go to sleep I was so tired.
>
> CECILIA HERNANDEZ, VILLA DÍAZ ORDAZ, SUMMER 2001

Understanding the give-and-take between the individual and his or her household is critical to comprehending what migration means for rural Oaxacans. The household is the fundamental social unit for most rural Oaxacans (Cook and Binford 1990; Selby 1974). Although an individual may be smart, successful, and well positioned in the local system, his or her household and its place in local society define that person's essential identity.

The household establishes a foundation upon which the individual can build success. The members of a household and the developmental stage of a household are also crucial to success. Meyer Fortes (1971, 4–5) stated that households follow a development cycle, and he used the idea to describe how the domestic unit changes over time, from its founding and expansion to its dispersion and replacement. Richard Wilk (1991) further developed the household concept, arguing that it is an adaptive structure that allows a domestic group to face challenges over time. Borrowing from both scholars, we can follow rural Oaxacan households as they change over time and adapt to the opportunities that the global market creates—including migration.

First, larger households—that is, households with more members—were more likely to include migrants. Households in the central valleys were typically organized around nuclear families that averaged five members (two adults and three children). Household size ranged from a low of one (six households that included older widows and widowers) to a family with sixteen members (two adults and fourteen children). Migrants were more common in larger households, although households with five to seven members constituted 56% of the migrants we identified. Additionally, more mature households—that is, households headed by older members—were also more likely to include migrants.[3]

The experiences of Marco Villas (thirty-five years old) and his household illustrate how the domestic cycle affects decision making and outcomes. Marco grew up in Santa Ana del Valle with his mother and three older brothers. His maternal uncle, Antonio Méndez, took on much of the burden of fatherhood following the sudden death of his father, as did Marco's eldest brother, Othón. Antonio and Othón (close in age and now in their late fifties) both migrated to the United States in the 1970s, and both earned green cards through the Immigration Reform and Control Act (IRCA) reforms that took place in the mid-1980s.[4]

Once the men earned their green cards and it became easier to move between Mexico and the United States, the pair brought Marco to the United States (as well as Antonio's two sons). In the United States, Marco and his cousins joined Othón and Antonio to work in seasonal agriculture. Over the three years that Marco stayed with his uncle and brother, he attended school sporadically and was able to become fluent in English. He returned the earnings that he was able to save to his mother in Santa Ana. She used the money to cover the costs of home improvements and to care for Marco's younger half-brother and half-sister, Rosa. In 1999, Rosa opened a small café in a remodeled room. The café was open almost daily, although its hours were sporadic. Rosa tended to serve construction workers who were in town and working on road and building projects.

In 1990, after three years of working in the United States, Marco returned to Santa Ana. Once home, he went back to farming and joined his mother in textile production. He also began a romance with a young woman who became his wife in 1991. In 1992 their first child was born. Marco described feeling that he was being pulled in several directions by his mother and his young wife and child. His mother counted on him to continue farming her land and to manage his brother's holdings. His brother described this as the debt Marco owed him for bringing him to the United States in 1987. Feeling rather desperate, Marco decided to return to the United States and work to earn the money he needed to build his own home and establish an independent household apart from his mother, brother, and uncle.

A tense period ensued during which accusations of improper behavior flew. Othón accused Marco of misusing money that he had sent to their mother between 1990 and 1993. He pointed to building supplies that Marco used in the construction of his home and declared, "I bought that rebar. It was for my house! And what thanks do I get? Nothing. I taught him [Marco] how to speak English; I brought him to the United States. I gave him everything, and this is what I get!"

Marco saw things differently. "I worked hard for them," he said. "I shared everything, and I have nothing to show for those years. Now I have a family [of four children by 2000], and I cannot ignore them!"

Marco returned to the United States in 1994 and began a three-year sojourn during which he worked in a series of restaurants in and around Los Angeles and Santa Monica, California. He moved between a series of apartments, one owned by Antonio, a second by a cousin. He was able to save some money and transferred it to his wife, María, in Santa Ana del Valle. By 1996 the couple had saved enough to complete a small, one-room home of concrete and brick, with a finished floor. The kitchen was typical for the community, a cane room with a thatch roof built to one side of the permanent structure.

In 1997, Marco was home, and he stayed long enough to complete the demands made on him by local authorities to spend a year contributing *servicio* in the community's *cargo* system. He spent the year as a member of a minor civil *cargo, alumbrado público* (the committee that maintains the town's streetlights). Upon completion of his duties, he left again for the United States. This time, he moved to a small town in Colorado. He lived with his younger sister, who had migrated with her husband and was living permanently in the United States.

Marco worked two restaurant jobs between 1998 and 2000. His skills in the kitchen—and, more important, his ability to serve as a translator for the largely Mexican staff and North American owners—worked to Marco's advantage. He quickly moved up the ladder from dishwasher to assistant manager. He left in the autumn of 2000 with an open invitation to return whenever he liked. During an interview in 2001, he described his experiences and commented on the future:

> It isn't easy living in the United States. I missed my family and my children, and I was away for too long. I saw things in Colorado that were unbelievable. My cousin was a security guard at a plant in town. One night he didn't feel well, so he asked this other guy [another Mexican from Oaxaca, but not from Santa Ana] to take his shift. They switched, and that

> guy was shot and killed during a robbery. That was when I started to think that it was really time to come home. It just isn't worth it, is it? What if you do this and work hard and then . . . I have my children, my home. What would be the point?
>
> MARCO VILLAS, SANTA ANA DEL VALLE, SUMMER 2001

By the summer of 2002, when I returned to Marco's home, most of the tensions between Marco and his brother had dissipated. A fence that Othón had built to divide Marco's homestead from his own was gone. Marco had added a finished second floor to his home, and the brothers had completed a deep well for both families to use. Marco's younger sister remains in the United States, where she has been for three years, and her husband works in the restaurant that Marco managed.

Marco described himself as content, and given the events of the autumn of 2001 in the United States, he had little desire to cross the border and return to his job in Colorado. In any case, he says, he cannot leave for at least a year, for he has a new *cargo* that began in January 2002. He is the treasurer for the public school attended by his daughter. The family has some money saved (invested in several pigs and goats), and he is producing textiles for sale locally.[5] His eldest son, who turned ten in 2002, is part of the community's dance troupe, their middle daughter is entering first grade, and their youngest son and daughter, four and two years old, respectively, are busy around the house. Marco thinks he may return to the United States in a few more years as his children get older and demand more toys. He also wants to buy a computer, but it is hard to find local work that will pay the wages needed for a big-ticket purchase like a computer. However, for the moment, Marco is happy to stay home, to weave, and to enjoy his family and his home, which is nearing completion and will include a modern kitchen with a refrigerator and a gas stove.

Most young rural Oaxacans face a series of challenges as they organize their new households. The young household has to be provisioned. Its members need to establish an identity in the community. Children must be cared for, and requirements for community service must be met. These challenges can easily overwhelm any one member of a domestic group. However, in general the members of rural Oaxacan households pool their resources and their efforts to cover the costs of daily maintenance, meet the demands of community participation, and save for emergencies and entertainment.

Selling produce and seeds in Tlacolula. Author photo.

Pooling within the household is crucial to the domestic unit's survival and health over time and space. Households that manage on the income and efforts of a single individual are rare in the central valleys. In fact, only 7% of the households we surveyed for this study were supported by a single worker. Generally, both male and female heads of a household contributed to the domestic group's well-being over time, and most households depended upon members combining work. Thirty-one percent of the households we surveyed combined two kinds of work, 28% combined at least three different jobs, 18% combined four possible jobs and 15% combined five or more possible jobs. Typically, farming and domestic work were the two most important activities in the household. The energy and efforts of children complimented the work of the household heads. Children began work at a young age and were expected to contribute to the well-being of the group without complaint (Leslie 1960; Nader 1990).

Given the importance of pooling to a household's success, it should be of little surprise that migration typically fits as one strategy among many that the members of a domestic group depend upon. Migration is, however, not an end in itself. Households did not view migration as a replacement for hard work. Rather, migration was a strategic move—one that allowed a household to access new work opportunities and supplement other local activities.

We found only one household whose members described themselves as fully supported by migrants. In this case, two brothers supported their wives, who were sisters and lived in a single household in Guadalupe Etla. The brothers lived in Mexico City, where they worked as elevator repairmen. The brothers had left Guadalupe Etla in the 1960s. Once settled in Mexico City, they entered a technical training program and found work as elevator service technicians. The brothers brought their wives to Mexico City, and each couple had three children. As their children grew and entered school, the sisters entered the workforce. One sister worked as a clerk, and the other took in sewing to supplement her husband's wages. The families remained intact and in Mexico City until the early 1990s. Doña Florencia described the changes that occurred once her children had left their natal home:

> I never liked Mexico City. It was noisy and dirty, I always missed home, and frankly, I was tired of my husband always bothering me [*laughs*]. So, Cecilia [her sister] and I, we came home and bought this house, and we are really happy. Our husbands send us plenty of money, and they come to visit once or twice a year, but really we are just happy to be left alone. We have this little store [a small *tienda* selling candies], and that keeps us happy. This is our town, and I'm glad we're home.
>
> FLORENCIA MALDONADO, GUADALUPE ETLA, SUMMER 2000

This was not a typical example, but it clearly showed how a household can change over time. The sisters were important contributors to the success of their households as they grew. Even though their husbands continued to support them (and their home is beautiful and large), the sisters continued to work, not only because they wanted to supplement their budgets with funds under their immediate control but also because a person who does not work is considered lazy in Oaxaca.

Finally, as we think about households, it is important to understand that although men dominate migration, women also move internally and to the United States. Figure 1.1 shows the number of men and women who

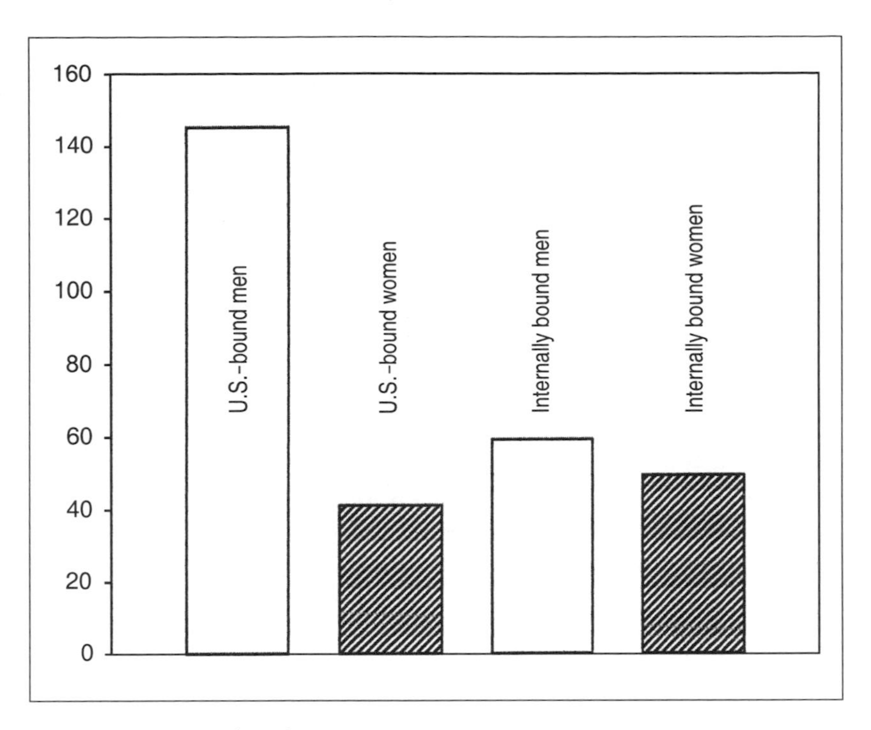

FIGURE 1.1. *Gender and migration.*

migrated to the United States and to internal destinations from sending communities in the central valleys.

Men constituted nearly 80% of the migrants bound for the United States. Internal migrations were more balanced in terms of gender: 51% of internal movers were men, 49% were women. The differences in internal and U.S.-bound migration rates were not surprising. Such differences have been documented by Reichert and Massey (1980) in their analysis of migration in Michoacán, by Donato (1993), and most recently by Curran and Rivero-Fuentes (2003) in their discussion of gendered networks and flows.

Women who traveled to the United States followed patterns that paralleled those of their male counterparts. However, whereas many of the men we talked to migrated as young household heads, most women migrated as daughters and supported their natal homes. Like men, women followed relatives and friends to their destinations, and 68% depended upon such networks (62% of men followed these networks).

Women were likely as well to follow men to the United States, and 60% of all the women who migrated to the United States came from a household that had sent a male member across the border. On the other hand, only 17% of the men identified came from households from which women were the first migrants. Women were generally a little younger than men when they first migrated (ages twenty and twenty-one, respectively, on average), and women remitted about half as much as their male counterparts (a topic discussed further in chapter 4).

At the center of a household's survival strategies are farming and domestic work. Producing maize, beans, and other vegetables for self-consumption is critical to most rural households, and 73% of the households we surveyed included members that participate in some kind of farm labor at home. From 1999 through 2001, households harvested an average of a six-month supply of maize, and 27% of households reported that they grew twelve-month supplies of maize on their plots.[6]

Male household heads handle much of the farming with the assistance of their sons. Households will sometimes hire help to work land, and the occasional migrant will let a nonmigrant farm a family plot *por la mitad* (for half of the harvest), following a sharecropping model. While men focus on farming for self-consumption and perhaps limited sales on the side, female household heads maintain the home and participate in the local labor market. We found that women often discounted their work as unimportant in the maintenance of their households over time. However, the work of these women was critical to the success of their households. *Tortilleras,* women who sell tortillas, earned an average of 50 pesos a day and worked from two to four days a week. The money their work generated was critical to households that must cover the expenses of food, schooling, utilities, and leisure. In the migrant household, a woman's earnings from the sale of tortillas made a substantial difference in the money that the domestic group saved and used for home improvements or investments rather than daily expenses.

Well-paying wage work is not prevalent in rural communities in Oaxaca, and certainly one force driving migration is the quest for good wages by individuals who must support the increasing demand for goods and services by their families and households. Typical wage work in the region includes construction labor for men and domestic work and sales for women. We found that older men and younger women were most likely to travel into Oaxaca City for work in construction and service. Professionals (individuals employed in management and careers that demanded advanced training) were evenly divided between men and women, and in general the families of these professionals did not depend upon migration.

Households combine their pooled resources with a series of communal

Women selling tejate *(a corn drink) in the market, May 2002. Photograph by Margaret Fox; reproduced with permission.*

practices through which the majority of rural Oaxacans create their identity. In addition to kin, fictive kin, and *compadrazgo* (godparent) relationships, rural Oaxacans participate in *tequio, servicio, cooperación,* and, for those rural Oaxacans who are indigenous, *guelaguetza* (reciprocal exchanges).[7]

Tequio is communal labor that households must provide when asked and in return for community membership (Cohen 1999; Nader 1990). We were able to collect information on *tequio* from 352 households in six communities, and we discovered that 74% of the households volunteered for work.

Tequio crosses ethnic and class lines, with volunteers coming from both indigenous and mestizo households and from both wealthy and poor households. Migrant and nonmigrant households also participate at equal levels, with the majority of both groups sending volunteers to work on *tequio.*

Servicio is the voluntary service that all households must provide to community government. Better known as the *cargo* system, *servicio* is a system of hierarchically ranked positions in a variety of civil, political, and religious committees (Cancian 1965, 1990; Chance 1990; Stephen 1991). Committees range from the powerful *comite del pueblo* (headed by the community's president and in charge of most village affairs), *bienes comunales* (community resources), and the *comite del templo* (in charge of the community's church and ritual life) to mundane committees, which have multiplied as additional services appear.

In the six communities for which we collected complete histories of household *cargo* service, we found that 47% of all households sent members to perform *servicio.* Two mestizo communities, Guadalupe Etla and San Martín Tilcajete, had slightly lower rates of participation (particularly San Martín Tilcajete), but San Juan del Estado, also a mestizo community, shared the highest rate of participation (60%) with San Juan Guelavia, a Zapotec-speaking community.

I assumed that migration would place pressure on *servicio* and therefore would lead to a decline in the participation of households in the *cargo* system. However, 46% of migrant households said they sent members to fill *cargo* positions. It appears that community traditions and the demands of service that ask households to participate voluntarily on a one-year-on, three-years-off cycle are enough to maintain the system.[8]

Cooperación is the third plank upon which communal life is built in rural Oaxaca. Households are assessed fees throughout the year to cover the expenses that are associated with rural development and community celebrations.

Ninety-eight percent of the households we surveyed reported that they had paid *cooperación* in the last year. Payments ranged from the trivial (10 pesos) to the substantial (300 pesos). Payments were determined by the costs of the event or project and the ability of the households to pay. Households that lacked incomes were not assessed *cooperación* to the same degree as those households that could pay more. However, many households that paid less than average for *cooperación* mentioned that they often served extra *tequio* to cover the difference.

Cooperación is growing in importance in relation to migration, but this pattern is historically rooted in the arrival of market capitalism and wage labor in the region in the early to mid-twentieth century (see Kearney 1995). Smith (1998) notes that migrants who had moved to the United States from home communities in the state of Puebla organized funds to cover the expenses of community development projects. In particular, he notes that these migrants covered the costs associated with building sewer systems in sending communities. Kearney (2000) finds much the same patterns among Mixtec migrants, who participated in migrant hometown associations to support economic development and political activism at home (see also Rivera-Salgado 1999). We have not found any patterns that are quite so formal in the central valleys, but many households told us they could not afford the costs of *cooperación* without the funds that migrants remit from the United States (see Orozco 2002).

Guelaguetza is found throughout the valleys but is typical to indigenous communities, including Santa María Guelacé, San Juan Guelavia, and Santa Ana del Valle. *Guelaguetza* is a Zapotec term that describes the formalized reciprocal exchanges of goods, money, and services between households. Households track their *guelaguetza* and participation—that is, gift giving—through time and note most of their activities in formal *guelaguetza* books. Participation in *guelaguetza* is one way in which a household enhances its social status in a community. Members of 40% of the households in three indigenous communities—San Juan Guelavia, Santa María Guelacé, and San Juan del Río—described *guelaguetza* as an important activity and crucial to their daily welfare. In mestizo communities, fewer households identified specific *guelaguetza* relationships but often maintained less formalized ties to other households.

Indigenous households establish *guelaguetza* relationships around marriage ceremonies and rituals, including *mayordomías* (sponsorship of saints' day celebrations) and other life-cycle celebrations. Households use their *guelaguetza* relationships for support and to make ends meet—and they keep a careful tally of their *guelaguetza* commitments, both what they are owed and what they owe others. A couple may use *guelaguetza* exchanges to cover labor on a home. More typically, households use *guelaguetza* to meet the labor required for a fiesta (a wedding or a saint's day celebration) and to gather the food that will be consumed by guests, which at a standard fiesta can amount to hundreds of people (see Stephen 1991).

The young household is largely defined by the debts it owes to its supporters. This is particularly true for indigenous households that have received a great deal of help as they begin their social life as a unit. *Guelaguetza* must be repaid—the debts can be carried for years, but they are not forgotten. Furthermore, the debts can be recalled at any time. Thus, many

Mother and daughters, Guadalupe Etla. Author photo.

young families feel quite burdened by these costs. Current patterns among households indicate that reciprocal ties remain critical to rural households, and few households refuse support or reject participating in reciprocal exchanges. Even in nonindigenous communities, young families incur debts as they establish themselves and define their identities. The burden of *servicio* places additional strain on the young household's resources, as does the birth of children.[9]

The mature household, on the other hand, may be indebted to other households, but it will likely hold *guelaguetza* debts as well. It has an identity in the community that is defined by years of service, and because its resources are not fully focused on sustaining children and covering the expense of their education, it can begin to move some of its resources into other areas. For example, the household might choose to invest in land or agricultural supplies or even to open a small business. Domestic groups who have older children and strong ties to other households and are active in the social life of the village (participating in the community's civil or religious hierarchies) will likely have more options for the strategic use of incomes and remittances than the domestic group that must struggle to feed young children and holds few social ties to other households.

The issue of a household's status, both as an integrated unit and as part of the community, returns us to the question, why use a household model and not a model focused on the decisions and desires of the individual? As I noted, the household is the fundamental or essential unit through which rural Oaxacans create a sense of identity and belonging in their communities. By participating in *tequio* and *servicio* and by paying *cooperación,* a household creates a social identity that translates into status and prestige. Wealth, whether it is earned locally or in the United States, makes people envious, but status comes from using that wealth (or at least some of it) in service to the community.

A good example of how wealth serves the community is found in our interview with the *presidente municipal* (community president and the head of the *comite del pueblo*) in San Martín Tilcajete. We had some difficulty when we initially presented our idea of a survey to the *presidente.* First, he said no and that we could not enter the town. However, other members of the *comite* quickly challenged his decision. An argument ensued. The *presidente* asked that we give him detailed information concerning the incomes for each household we visited in the community. We responded that we could not ethically comply with his request but would give him a summary of our findings.

Then the *presidente* accused members of his *comite* of malfeasance. He argued that at least two members of the *comite* had sent their children to the United States, and those members were not supporting the town. In other words, the money sent home by these boys served their households' own interest and did not support the community. Accepting his challenge, the secretary of the community responded, "My sons are in the United States, but they help me. They send me US$200 a month so that I can work with you!" The argument continued for a short time. The *presidente* finally agreed that we could conduct our surveys and that he did not in fact need detailed data on the incomes of households in the village. The moment may seem rather mundane and the argument almost comical, but it is indicative of how money made in wage labor and migration is seen locally. Money corrupts traditional practices unless it is used to serve those practices. Using at least some resources to support communal affairs, households are able to migrate, seek wage labor in Oaxaca City, and use their earnings to pursue their own and their household's desires (see Cohen 1999; Greenberg 1995).

Migration sits at the intersection of these processes. It is rooted in household decisions and influenced by community demands. Nevertheless, a migrant—that is, an individual—makes the final decision. The individual decides whether he or she will follow tradition and embrace the household and its goals or will turn his or her back on the group and set out for a new life. The community also cannot demand that a migrant or a migrant household participate in its civil society. A community's leaders can sanction households that choose to ignore the requirements of membership, and sanctions can be as serious as a household's expulsion from the community. However, a household whose members choose not to participate in a community's ritual or civil life have effectively made that choice; expulsion may be little more than the physical manifestation of a "done deal." The point is that for all of the pressure that a household can exert upon its members and that a community can exert upon its constituent households (whether those individuals and households are physically in the community or living away from the community), it is only because the individuals and households choose to participate that the system works. Rural Oaxacans, as I hope will become clear, are deeply committed to their households and their communities. Much of the future for the region and the people who live there will be determined not by migration but by whether that commitment continues.

Two HISTORY, TRAJECTORY, AND PROCESS IN OAXACAN MIGRATION

Migration is not a decision made in haste. Families and households plan for the migrations of their members and anticipate the outcomes of the moves. Migration is a part of local history, and as was outlined in the introduction, it is one way in which a household is able to meet the challenges of daily life. Migration has a history, and movement follows a trajectory, building slowly over time, spiking during economic crisis at home, and declining in response to changes in opportunity, reception, and need. To understand migration in the present, we must follow its development over time. To capture what the past means, I begin in the present, and with events in 1992–1993 that focused my interests on migration.

For a year I lived in Santa Ana del Valle, a Zapotec-speaking community of about three thousand artisans and farmers, beginning in the summer of 1992 (Cohen 1999). My goal was to understand how Santañeros (the people of Santa Ana) adapted cooperative and reciprocal relationships to the challenges of their increasing incorporation into the global capitalist market system. Although I knew that the issue of migration might come up, I had not anticipated that it would so fill the discussions that I had with friends and informants throughout the year. The moment that set in motion the project you are now reading about occurred in January 1993, immediately after the community celebrated its *patrona* (patron saint), a celebration that included fiestas, masses, *mayordomías,* dances, large banquets, and a rodeo.

After the celebration, a large number of men from the community migrated to destinations in the United States, such as Santa Monica, California, and to jobs in the service industry, construction, and agriculture. Simultaneously, men I had only heard about in stories returned to their families. They came home to farm, to serve in the *cargo* system, to renew friendships, and, for some, to meet children who had not yet been born when they left.

Several migrants who were leaving for the United States asked for rides to the bus station in Oaxaca (which I supplied, using the time to learn more about their motivations). I took one young Santañero, Roman García, to Oaxaca City's airport—he was flying to Tijuana, just across the border from San Diego, to meet his brother. His brother had a green card and lived full-time in Santa Monica, California, where he worked in a Chinese restaurant. He drove to Tijuana, picked up Roman, and brought him to the apartment he shared with several other Santañeros. Roman planned to stay in the United States for at least six months (he remained for nearly two years) and to work alongside his brother as a busboy in the restaurant. Roman wanted to earn enough money to outfit his kitchen. He was able to do that, and he and his wife were also able to save enough of his remittances to renovate most of their home—building a modern bathroom in addition.

My *patrón* (my sponsor in Santa Ana), Don Mario, and his wife, Doña Christina, also left for the United States in early February. Don Mario and Doña Christina had not seen their three sons and two daughters for more than two years (a fourth son lived with them in Santa Ana, although by 2002 he was living in the United States as well). They had U.S.-born grandchildren that they had yet to meet and whose baptisms were eminent. Don Mario also needed money. He had invested much of his savings to cover the costs of cement and rebar that he used to renovate his home. More costly were the two weddings in which he and Christina served as *padrinos* (godparents) for the newlyweds. Rural Oaxacans are traditional Catholics, and social roles such as the role of godparents are crucial to the maintenance of community (see Nutini 1984).

A person has several godparents, who serve in various roles throughout the lives of their *ahijados* (godchildren). The most important godparents a child has are the *padrinos del bautismo* (godparents who sponsor and cover the costs of a baptismal celebration). *Padrinos del bautismo* support the spiritual and corporal well-being of their godchild in the event that the natural parents die. The *padrinos* act as guardians, but they often become confidants and typically support their *ahijados* through troubled times—for example, when birth parents cannot meet wedding expenses, including the purchase of a wedding chest or armoire. Minor *padrinos* and other friends and associates spend thousands of dollars on baptisms and weddings, helping to cover the costs of food, music, clothes, and ritual services. Don Mario and Doña Christina served as *padrinos* at the baptism of a neighbor's child and later in the same month at the wedding of their niece. They spent a great deal of money first to purchase the baptismal clothing for their *ahijado* and to help cover the costs of the Mass and celebration, and they contributed to a wedding, covering the costs of food that served about a hundred guests.

Don Mario was feeling the pinch. Most of his savings went to his kitchen project and the expenses of the baptism and the wedding. Over breakfast of *atole* (corn milk), sweet bread, and tortillas one morning, he began talking about a trip to the United States. I discovered that he and Doña Christina had begun planning that she would join her husband to visit their children and grandchildren. A solitary trip for Don Mario (one that he might have used to earn some dollars) became a vacation for him and Doña Christina.

This would be the first time that Doña Christina had left the community for more than a day. For Don Mario, it was just another trip to the United States and followed a series of sojourns that began in the 1950s, when he first joined the migrants streaming north to the United States as a bracero. Don Mario served as a bracero on four different occasions, finding legal work as a farmhand. After the program ended, he continued traveling to the United States and made four more trips with destinations throughout the western and northwestern parts of the country. He worked as a gardener, a fruit picker, and a construction worker. On his last trip he had found a position as a baker, working side by side with his sons.

In early February 1993, after weeks of discussion, Don Mario and Doña Christina got into my car so that I could drive them to the second-class bus station in the heart of Oaxaca City. Rogelio, the last of their children who still lived in Santa Ana, and a number of other relatives squeezed into the car to see them off. The couple carried a few days' worth of clothes in two old suitcases. Don Mario even packed his dress shoes, polished and black, for the trip. Doña Christina bought a new dress. The couple was able to secure visas and papers and would be traveling to the United States as tourists destined to see their children and grandchildren. They carried a large cardboard box filled with tortillas and *mole oaxaqueño,* a local sauce made with chocolate and chiles that is served with chicken at celebrations. Doña Christina would serve her *mole* at the baptism of their granddaughter in Los Angeles.

Don Mario and Doña Christina arrived in Los Angeles without encountering any delays at the border. They were met by their sons, who took them to one of their small apartments in Santa Monica. Several dozen people consumed the *mole* over the course of several days in celebration of the baptism of Angelica, their granddaughter. The celebration brought together Santañeros who lived in Los Angeles and Santa Monica. It was an opportunity for Don Mario and Doña Christina to provide details of local gossip and deliver the news of events in Santa Ana. It was also a moment for the community to come together in the United States without being afraid for the future, work prospects, or *la migra* (the U.S. Immigration and Naturalization Service).

Don Mario and Doña Christina traveled on short-term tourist visas, for which they had paid dearly, and they quickly moved in with their son Eduardo, his wife, María (also a Santañera), and their three young children, who had all been born in the United States.[1] Don Mario went to work the next week in a bakery that employed Eduardo and Don Mario's other sons, Felix and Julio. The three sons have green cards and live legally in the United States in adjoining apartments in Santa Monica. Together the four men worked daily. Doña Christina managed the home and helped with her grandchildren. The couple stayed in the United States for just a little more than a year, and they returned to Santa Ana in the spring of 1994 in time to begin planting for the coming growing season.

After their return, Don Mario and Doña Christina stayed in Santa Ana and did not see their sons or grandchildren again for more than five years. Eduardo came back to the village with one son in 2001 and spent four months at home, working beside his father. Together they laid pipe that connected Don Mario's home to Santa Ana's new sewer system. Eduardo's young son enjoyed visiting his grandparents and seeing the area, but he also missed home and was not enthusiastic about the rustic lifestyle that Santañeros lead.

In 2001, Don Mario and Doña Christina's granddaughter Ana married a boy whose parents were also migrants from Santa Ana. The boy's parents carried green cards and were in the United States legally, as were Ana's parents. The bride and groom had both been born in the United States and had grown up speaking both Spanish and English. They understood Zapotec and could even manage to speak a little, but it was largely the language of their parents and grandparents. Following a small church wedding in the United States, the young couple returned to Santa Ana for a much larger and traditional wedding celebration.

Don Mario and Doña Christina sponsored the event with the help of the groom's family and the support of households throughout the community that brought food, supplies, and money to help cover expenses. A small home was built for the couple on land that Don Mario owned just to the north of the main village and in a relatively new *colonia* (neighborhood) that sits above the town proper. The new one-room home is near three empty homes that belong to Don Mario's three sons.[2] The newlyweds spent a few weeks in town living in their new home, but they soon returned to California, where they reside permanently.

MEXICAN MIGRATION IN HISTORY

In chapter 1, I described the realities of life in Oaxaca and noted that it is a poor, rural state with limited economic opportunities. A growing population and a stagnant market for work combine with low wages to push rural Oaxacans to seek labor in national and international destinations, and migration has increased rapidly since the 1970s. Nevertheless, migration is not a new phenomenon. Oaxacans, like most rural Mexicans, have always migrated. Oaxacans are part of the history of contemporary U.S.-Mexican migration that dates back at least to the 1930s, when nearly 500,000 Mexican migrants lived in the United States (Verduzco Igartúa 1995). However, migration for rural Oaxacans and for most Mexicans in general is not just about making the decision to cross the border to the United States.

Rural Oaxacans engage in a number of moves that take them to distinct destinations. First are local moves that follow circuits or commutes between rural hometowns and Oaxaca City or some other urban center in the region. Typically, rural Oaxacans follow local circuits for regional employment opportunities and for education. San Pablo Huitzo and to a lesser degree San Juan del Estado attract local circuit movers, but in general the circuits we discovered in the central valleys took workers and students from their rural hometowns directly to Oaxaca City.

A second move that Oaxacans can make is to national destinations in growing urban centers and boomtowns within Mexico. Oaxacans have traveled to Tapachula, Chiapas; to towns along the U.S. frontier, like Tijuana, where they sometimes settle; and to tourist towns, including Cancún, Acapulco, and Huatulco. The majority continue to travel to traditional destinations such as Mexico City and find work in construction or service.

The majority of Oaxaca's migrants follow a third route, and like migrants from throughout Mexico, they make the trek to the United States, where most have settled in Southern California. A second large Zapotec community is well settled in Chicago. There are also new destinations for migrants from the central valleys (see Durand et al. 2000). For example, a large group of migrants from Santa María Guelacé has settled in Poughkeepsie, New York.[3] A second destination for migrants from San Juan del Estado and Santa María Guelacé is northern New Jersey and southeastern Pennsylvania. Migrants travel to the former for domestic, service, and construction work, whereas the latter supplies agricultural jobs on mushroom farms.

A fourth strategy followed by some central valley Oaxacans is to com-

Guadalupe Etla's main street, July 2002. Author photo.

bine national and international migration (Conway and Cohen 2002), but only a little more than 7% of the households we surveyed had made such decisions. Most rural Oaxacan migrants choose one destination, either national or international, and that is where they go. Repeat migrations tend to follow well-used paths, and migrants usually return to destinations where they found some success rather than confronting the risks of a new destination.

MIGRATION IN OAXACA'S HISTORY

The last century of Mexican migration is divided into three more or less distinctive phases.[4] The first period preceded the Mexican Revolution (1910–1921), when Mexicans sought refuge from fighting at home by crossing the border. Many of these migrants worked in industry or for railroad lines, and many stayed in the United States for extended periods before returning to Mexico (Monto 1994, 54). This pattern remained consistent through the First World War and the organization of the first bracero program, which ran from 1917 to 1923 (Monto 1994, 54). The bracero program supplemented U.S. labor shortages as the involvement of the United States in the war increased. Gamio (1931, 13) estimated that the majority of the migrants during this period (54%) were from Mexico's west and central states of Michoacán, Guanajuato, and Jalisco. This pattern continued through the Great Depression, when economic collapse in the United States led to the forcible return of nearly 500,000 Mexicans to their homeland (Craig 1971).

Migration through the early decades of the twentieth century was also marked by short-term seasonal moves that emphasized regional or national destinations. Migrants traveled to internal destinations for temporary work in plantations and fields and for work in road and construction projects throughout Mexico (Iszaevich 1988).

The second phase of migration begins after a binational agreement between the United States and Mexico inaugurated a second bracero program in 1942. The agreement established a federally mandated program to cover labor shortages in the United States that coincided with its growing involvement in the Second World War. The program guaranteed Mexican men (and only men) the right to work in the United States under formal short-term contracts that specified rights to food, housing, medical care, fixed pay, and funds to cover returns to Mexico. The U.S. government played the role of employer and assumed that U.S. farm and plant managers would comply with the program's regulations (Monto 1994, 56). The success of the program was evident in the increasing numbers of men who participated (rising to more than 400,000 in the late 1950s) and the value of remittances those men returned to Mexico (Craig 1993; Massey 1987; Monto 1994).[5]

The bracero program was unfortunately plagued with problems. Farm labor replaced higher-paying industrial jobs, while access to permits grew more difficult (Monto 1994). According to Foster (1979), municipal leaders in Tzintzuntzan, Michoacán, sold bracero contracts to the highest bidders. At the same time, U.S. farm owners and growers often hired illegal migrants who would work for lower wages than formally contracted braceros. Monto (1994, 57) notes that even as contracted bracero workers entered the United States in increasing numbers, the total number of illegal immigrants apprehended by the U.S. Immigration and Naturalization Service skyrocketed as well. With illegal entries to the United States rising and migrant workers realizing they could effectively circumvent the bracero program and find work without contracts, the project ended in 1966 (Massey 1987, 55).[6]

The most recent phase of movement started when the bracero program ended. Mexican migrants continued to move across the border and to travel to internal destinations, as they had for decades. In fact, although the esti-

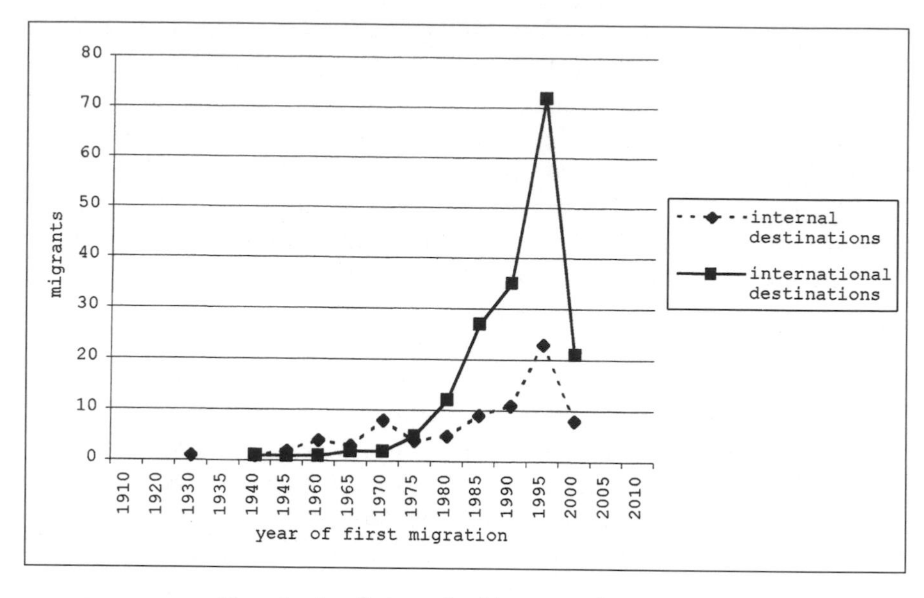

FIGURE 2.1. *First migrations for internal and international movers.*

mates of Mexican-born migrants living in the United States range widely, it is known that hundreds of thousands of Mexicans were moving back and forth between their home communities and settlements in the United States, and the majority of these migrants were undocumented (Van Hook and Bean 1998). The flow of migrants out of Oaxaca remained relatively low throughout the late 1960s and the 1970s. In fact, the number of new migrants leaving for internal migration paralleled and sometimes dwarfed the number of migrants leaving for international destinations from central valley communities until the late 1970s (figure 2.1). Migration to the United States began its rapid rise following a series of economic crises in Mexico during the 1980s (Corbett et al. 1992; Hulshof 1991). Nevertheless, the majority of migrants in our study did not leave for their first sojourns until the mid-1990s, and half of all movers left the United States after 1995.

EARLY MOVERS IN OAXACA

In the first half of the twentieth century, Oaxacans typically migrated internally, and the majority of moves were to nearby towns and cities where work could be found.[7] Local circuits took men from Villa Díaz

Ordaz, San Juan Guelavia, and Santa Ana del Valle to Tlacolula, where they could find work in fields owned by powerful families like the Chagoyas. Traveling to Oaxaca to work or to sell produce, crafts, and goods was not common. As one elderly man from Villa Díaz Ordaz put it, "Oaxaca—oh, the city was a day's trip! We had to go to Tlacolula [walking], and then we would take the train. It was such an adventure. We would be gone all day."

Regional moves took Oaxacans to coastal plantations where they found seasonal labor. Sometimes this meant that the migrants would join in the harvest of crops like sugarcane. They would work through the season and then return home. Others found work as itinerant peddlers, selling goods to the migrant settlements during the harvest season. One older man described both options as difficult but worth the money. Don Valeriano García, an elderly Santañero, described his experiences during the 1940s when he traveled to Chiapas and worked as a vendor of *paletas* (frozen fruit bars):

Selling paletas *(frozen confections) in San Martín Tilcajete, May 2001. Author photo.*

TABLE 2.1 MIGRANT DESTINATIONS BY GENDER

	Internal movers	*International movers*	*Total migrants*
Males	81	252	333
Females	77	66	143
Gender unknown	46	64	110
Total	204	382	586

> In the mornings, my patron would give me my order to sell. I had my territory and my cart, and I would work my way through the town, calling out, *"Paletas, paletas!"* I'd work all day long, moving through the mountains. I did that for three summers, but it was too much.
>
> DON VALERIANO GARCÍA, SANTA ANA DEL VALLE, FEBRUARY 1993

Other Oaxacans sought wage labor in large and growing urban centers like Mexico City, always referred to as "el D.F."—the Distrito Federal, or Federal District (see Hirabayashi 1993). In the larger urban centers, rural Oaxacan men found work in construction and the service industry. Although men were the majority of migrants moving internally, women also engaged in migration and constituted nearly half of all migrants traveling within national boundaries (table 2.1). In particular, women found work as domestics (Iszaevich 1988, 191). Domestics, often called *sirvientas,* worked extremely hard, and although they were usually given room and board, they earned very little. The comments of Doña Amelia capture how difficult domestic work was:

> I spent almost thirty years working in Mexico City. Thirty years, but what was I to do? Once my dear husband died, I had no choice. I had my daughter to support, and she was so young. She was born shortly before my husband died. I left her with my mother and father, and I found a job in the D.F. I worked for the same family for thirty years! I cleaned for them, I cooked, I took care of them. But what do I have to show for my time? Nothing! I'm so stiff, and I suffer now. I couldn't keep working. So now I am home, my daughter and

> her husband take care of me, and I help where I can, but I didn't bring anything home. I couldn't save a thing or bring a thing home. Just this old sewing machine.
>
> DOÑA AMELIA HERNANDEZ, SAN JUAN DEL ESTADO, JUNE 2000

Many men also found occasional work closer to home on projects that included the Pan-American Highway. Don Valeriano García, who had spent time working in Chiapas, also worked on the highway. He commented on the time he spent working on a crew that prepared the grade for the Pan-American Highway as it wove through the central and southeastern mountains of Oaxaca:

> That was hard work. Three of us went to work on the crew. We were young and strong, and we joined the highway as it went through to the Isthmus [of Tehuantepec]. One day this guy from Tlacolula just disappeared over the edge—we never saw him again. It was dangerous work, but it paid well. We stayed for about a month working on the highway, and then we came home.
>
> DON VALERIANO GARCÍA, SANTA ANA DEL VALLE, MARCH 1993

Later still, Don Valeriano García was one of the first Santañeros to migrate to the United States, where he worked as a bracero. By the time I talked with him in 1993, his sons lived full-time in Santa Monica, California (in the same complex as Don Mario and Doña Christina's children), and he had grandchildren who had been born in the United States.

While men sought work regionally when they could, rural Oaxacan women were more likely to follow local circuits to Oaxaca City or internal migration routes to larger cities, where they found domestic work. Women from Santa María Guelacé commuted to Oaxaca to sell vegetables in local markets, while others followed the weekly market cycle that circles the central valleys (see Cook and Diskin 1976). Women from Guadalupe Etla sold cheese and milk in the city, and women from San Pedro Ixtlahuaca typically went to the city's main market two or three times a week to sell tortillas.[8]

OAXACAN MIGRATION AT MIDCENTURY

Migration trajectories changed for the nation following the establishment of the bracero program in 1942. The program permitted Mexicans to enter the United States legally, but for no more than ninety days at first. In total, 4.6 million legal contracts were organized during the bracero program, and although an average of 209,000 Mexicans entered the United States each year to work as braceros, only 12% of that total sought to remain there permanently (Verduzco and Unger 1998, 399).

Braceros were unevenly divided among Oaxacan communities. Iszaevich (1988, 192–193) notes that the community of Santa Cruz Etla included "a strong contingent of braceros" as well as internal migrants, while Santa María Atzompa sent no braceros to the United States. Teotitlán del Valle was the hometown of fifteen migrants living in the United States (none were identified by Iszaevich as having been braceros), while nearly half the male population of San Lucas Quiaviní were in the United States (again none were identified as braceros). In any case, Oaxacans remained a small part of the stream of Mexicans who found work through the bracero program (approximately 2.9% in 1962; pers. comm., Douglas Massey).

Oaxacan braceros worked at various jobs in agriculture and industry. Don José Sánchez, a man in his early fifties from Villa Díaz Ordaz, made four trips to various places in the southwestern United States as a bracero. In an interview in May 2001 he recalled, "I loved my work in the United States. The work was good, and everything was secure. I didn't have to worry like everyone does today." Others described how hard they worked on their contracts. Nevertheless, former braceros generally looked back on the time they spent in the United States as largely positive. Often they would mention that the biggest difference today is not so much the work as the dangers that come with crossing the border without documentation.

Internal migration rose throughout the 1950s, 1960s, and 1970s. Men described their work and time spent in Mexico City in positive terms as well. Several informants talked about the skills they acquired in Mexico City. One man from Guadalupe Etla apprenticed as a butcher in the D.F., married a young woman, and worked in a butcher shop for a decade. Later he returned home to Guadalupe Etla, where he opened his own shop. In the fall of 1999 he retired and devoted himself to his hobbies—rebuilding cars and raising tropical fish.

The opportunities and benefits that could be had in the D.F. in the 1970s were amazing, particularly when compared with those of rural Oaxaca. Most rural communities lacked electricity until the late 1970s; sewers and

Women selling tortillas in the Tlacolula market, May 2002. Photograph by Margaret Fox; reproduced with permission.

piped water were unheard of. The local economy was simply too sparse to support entrepreneurial activities, educational advancement, and the like.

While men were beginning to move in larger numbers to the United States, both men and women followed local circuits, commuting to work and to sell produce, dairy products, and crafts in Oaxaca City and other centers. People from Guadalupe Etla, San Pedro Ixtlahuaca, and Santa María Guelacé followed the circuits that their parents and grandparents had established earlier.

Señora Inés Martínez has sold tortillas in Oaxaca's markets for decades. While we talked one afternoon in her home in San Pedro Ixtlahuaca, Señora Martínez busied herself with making large maize tortillas that are typical for Oaxaca. She took a ball of masa (cornmeal) from her metate (grinding stone) and placed it into her tortilla press. She made two full presses on one side, then turned the tortilla over for a second pressing. Finally, she laid the tortilla on her *comal* (clay cooking surface), where it would quickly toast. She stacked the finished tortillas in a reed basket lined with a plastic bag. When she was done, she would take the filled basket to Oaxaca City, where she would sell her goods at the 20 de Noviembre market in the center of town. As she worked, she described her experiences:

> I sell tortillas two and sometimes three times a week. When I was younger, I always went three times a week, but now I am not as able—I'm fifty-six, you know. . . . I would get up early—maybe five o'clock in the morning!—and start making tortillas. Sometimes my daughters would help me. We would work and work. Then I would take my tortillas and walk to the city. It would take some time, but there were always other women to walk with. Sometimes I would get a ride on a cart, but most of the time I just walked. I would get to the city market to sell my tortillas for *comida* [she used her earnings to buy groceries for the midday meal]. Everybody would buy my tortillas. Then I would walk all the way home. Today I'm still selling my tortillas, but I take the bus. It is only about a ten-minute ride now! Can you believe that? I used to walk and walk, but now it is so easy with the bus and the taxis.
>
> SEÑORA INÉS MARTÍNEZ, SAN PEDRO IXTLAHUACA, JUNE 2001

For a day in the market, Señora Martínez can usually earn about 50 pesos, and on a good day, nearly 100 pesos (approximately US$5–10). It might seem that Señora Martínez got very little for the time, energy, and effort she invested in making, trucking, and selling her tortillas. However, the money she earned was critical to the success and health of her household. Over the years, she has pooled her income from the sale of tortillas with the food her husband produced on 1.5 hectares of land and his occasional earnings in construction and as a day laborer. By pooling their resources, the couple ensured that their three children could complete their education. In fact, their son pursued an accounting degree at the Instituto Tecnológico de Oaxaca.

CONTEMPORARY MIGRATION IN RURAL OAXACA

Migration to the United States from Oaxaca increased rapidly and dramatically through the 1990s until by the year 2000 an average of 34% of a community's households had at least one migrant living across the border. Nevertheless, the United States is not the only destination available to rural Oaxacans. Figures from INEGI (2002b) suggest that 10% of Oaxaca City's workforce commute from surrounding communities. Other internal migrations also remain important. People from the central valleys of the state have migrated in the 1980s to Tapachula, Chiapas, a boomtown on the Mexican-Guatemalan border, and in the 1990s to Baja California for agricultural work (Rees and Coronel Ortiz 2002).

Oaxaca's tourist economy pulls workers to the city from throughout the central valleys. INEGI estimates that one in four workers in the city are employed in service and commerce, and the majority of these positions are related to tourism in the city (INEGI 1999, 5). Younger people travel to Oaxaca to train at the city's colleges and universities. San Pablo Huitzo has grown in importance as a local market center and now attracts some workers to its service economy. Guadalupe Etla and San Pedro Ixtlahuaca also attract new residents, as city dwellers seek homes in a more rural setting.

Through the 1990s, households continued to send members to national destinations and internal migration increased, although at a much-reduced rate in comparison with U.S.-bound migration. The sustained movement of rural Oaxacans to Mexico City, with its booming economy, began in the 1960s and 1970s in response to a series of changes in agrarian policies. First, policies that favored large-scale irrigation projects over family farms pressured small landholders to move away from agriculture (Warman 1978). Second, price controls on maize contributed to a 33% drop in the crop's market value between 1957 and 1973, which further pressured small local producers to seek new opportunities (Arizpe 1981, 631). Finally, an increase in job opportunities in urban centers became a powerful attractor, pulling rural Mexicans to cities like Guadalajara, the D.F., and, to lesser degree, regional centers like Oaxaca (Cornelius and Bustamante 1989; Downing 1979; Monto 1994).

Rural Oaxacans established satellite settlements in the D.F. as the economic boom continued. Hirabayashi (1983) documents the many associations that were organized by mountain Zapotec and Mixtec during the

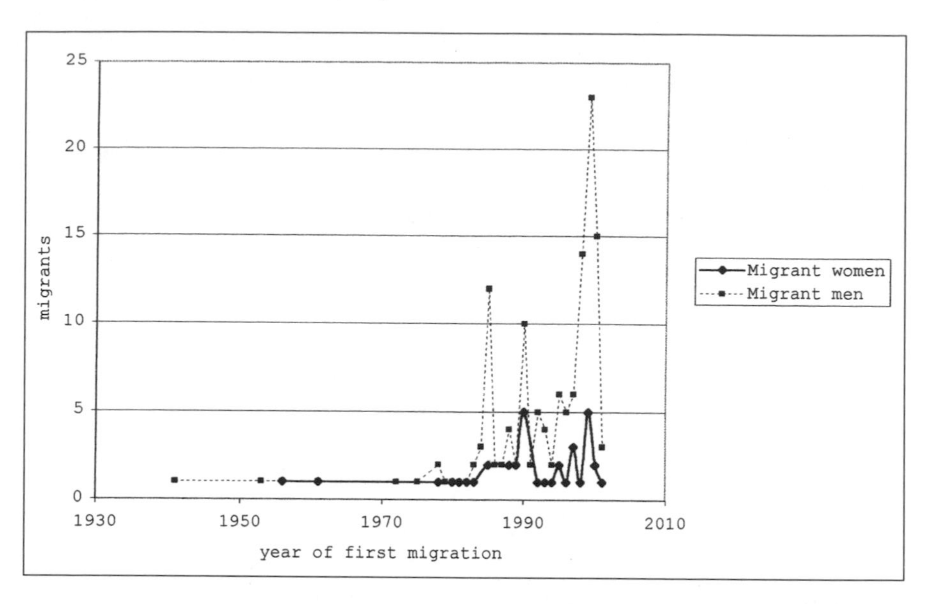

FIGURE 2.2. *First migrations to the United States by gender.*

1960s and 1970s. Pioneers settled first, and slowly their family and friends followed. As news of an individual's or a family's success filtered home, more migrants joined the pioneers. Soon, enough families from a community were living in the new settlement that it became self-sustaining. The birth of children and the marriage of individuals with locals further solidified the migrant settlement. However, as Hirabayashi (1993) notes, the ties that linked settlements in Mexico City with hometowns in Oaxaca did not fade with time. Instead, these networks, which he calls *paisanazgo* (neighborly ties) remained powerful and became a crucial resource for the success of the migrant.

We found a similar pattern in San Pablo Huitzo. A large community of expatriates from the village live full-time in Mexico City. These migrants remain tied to their hometown and make an annual pilgrimage to San Pablo for the community's fiestas. Typically, people from the D.F. sponsor at least one *mayordomía* in the town. They hire a priest and fill a caravan of buses to make the trek home to San Pablo.

First migration to the United States from the central valleys remained flat throughout the 1960s and early 1970s (see figure 2.1). However, the rate began to rise in 1978 and continued to grow through the 1980s, particularly among rural Oaxacan men (figure 2.2). First migrations spiked in 1984 and 1988, as Mexico endured economic crises. This pattern continued through the 1990s, with first sojourns to international destinations rising throughout the decade.

By the dawn of the twenty-first century, migration to the United States and Mexican destinations had reached a point where it was self-sustaining. Massey et al. (1994, 1496) describe this phenomenon as occurring when migration "acquires an internal momentum all its own . . . [and] becomes increasingly independent of the conditions that originally caused it." Such a process appears ongoing among central valley communities. The original impetus for migration—higher wages and regular work—had not changed. What had changed were the risks associated with migration. More than half of all migrants leaving central valley households had a direct connection to a migrant already living in the United States. In other words, migrants no longer crossed the border alone; instead they crossed with the knowledge that they had a place to stay and a support network available. Although the dangers of border crossings remain high, the networks that migrants have in their destinations mean an overall decline in risks. Declining risks does not mean that crossing the border is trouble free; rather it means that once the new or returned migrant has reached a receiving community, then finding work, a place to stay, and friends is much easier.

Oaxacans remain a small part of the overall stream of Mexicans migrating to the United States. INEGI (2001b) estimates that only about 7% of Oaxaca's population were involved in migration, whereas 27% of the population in Colima and just under 23% in Tamaulipas were involved. Nevertheless, internal migration and migration to the United States remain profoundly important to rural Oaxacan households and communities (see chapter 3). Yet the questions remain: why did migration take off so suddenly in the 1980s, and why did it rise so rapidly? To answer these questions, we need to look at three areas that contribute to the changes in migration—geography and technology; demography; and socioeconomic processes.

GEOGRAPHY, TECHNOLOGY, AND MIGRATION

During the first half of the twentieth century and even through the 1970s, traveling beyond one's home community was not an easy process for most rural Oaxacans. There were few finished roads, bus service was limited, and privately owned automobiles were largely unheard of. The impacts of the technological changes that have made travel throughout the valleys and migration so much easier are evident in this description of early migration in San Juan Guelavia by César Hipolito:

> You know, some men left here in the 1940s. Oh my, we just thought that they would never come home. We were just sure they were going to die out there in America. I didn't know how far it was to the United States. I didn't know how they went; they just left—we said good-bye and Godspeed, and watched them as they boarded the train.

Later in the same interview, Cesar described traveling locally before the advent of regular bus service:

> The train is how we went to the city. We almost never went, but when we did, we would wear our best clothes, would sit quietly, and I can remember being so scared of the city and the people. It was just such a big place! Sometimes we would take the oxen and cart to the city.
>
> CÉSAR HIPOLITO, SAN JUAN GUELAVIA, JULY 2000

The central valley communities share relatively better access to Oaxaca City and its markets than do communities throughout the rest of the state. Nevertheless, location and distance to the city do play a role in movement and migration outcomes. Historically, communities that are close to the city, including Guadalupe Etla, San Pedro Ixtlahuaca, and Santa María Guelacé share more ties to Oaxaca City and have a higher percentage of local commuters than distant communities like San Juan del Río, San Lorenzo Albarradas, and Santa Inés Yatzeche.

In Guadalupe Etla, San Pedro Ixtlahuaca, and Santa María Guelacé, nearly 40% of all migrant households include members who are also involved in local commutes. San Pablo Huitzo and San Juan del Estado are both farther from the city. However, both towns have direct access to the Pan-American Highway, and the quality of local roads and the large number of buses, taxis, and private automobiles moving back and forth to the city have led to large commuter populations as well (46% of Huitzo's movers and 40% of San Juan del Estado's movers). Men and women from these communities are involved in a variety of commutes to the city. Commuters include *tortilleras* from San Pedro Ixtlahuaca, farmers selling produce from Santa María Guelacé, and professionals from Guadalupe Etla,

San Juan del Estado, and San Pablo Huitzo. Day laborers, domestic workers, and students also travel in from each community.

Local commutes are more difficult for communities that lack good access to Oaxaca City. Not surprisingly, only a small percentage of movers from the three communities farthest from the city—San Juan del Río, San Lorenzo Albarradas, and Santa Inés Yatzeche—commute to the city (5, 20, and 10%, respectively). The odd community in this process is San Martín Tilcajete. Although it is near to Oaxaca City, only 18% of its population are involved in local commutes. In this case, the strength of the local economy that is built around the production and direct sale of Alebrijes means that there is less pressure to commute.

Geography is not directly important in the decisions to migrate to national and international destinations. Rather, concerns for local geography combine with personal desires, expected destinations, and the kinds of social resources that the potential migrant can bring to his or her decision making. The citizens of communities that are farther from the city may opt to participate in national or international migrations after weighing the costs of local commutes. For a farmer in a town like San Juan del Río, the options are limited. There are few local opportunities for work, and travel to Oaxaca City remains difficult. Thus, 75% of San Juan del Río's movers choose to migrate to the United States rather than migrating to a national destination or making a local commute. The situation is similar in Santa Inés Yatzeche, where 64% of the community's movers choose to migrate to the United States.

DEMOGRAPHY AND MIGRATION

Geography is only one variable that can affect outcomes. A second set of factors that influence migration decisions are demographic. Comparing the structure of rural Oaxacan families from the mid-twentieth century with contemporary family structure illustrates these changes. My sponsor in Santa Ana del Valle, Don Mario, was in his late fifties when I first met him in 1992. He was an only child, but simply because his parents' seven other children had died, all before the age of five. Don Mario was father to four sons and two daughters and a grandfather many times over. Increasing survival rates among children translated to an increase in family size and a rapid growth in the population, such that population density (that is, individuals per square kilometer) in these communities increased by 60%

(INEGI 2002a). One household in Guadalupe Etla included a couple with fourteen children who ranged in age from three to twenty-four years. Men joked that the household was blessed with too much good luck and would have been better off if at least a few of the children had died. On the other hand, this household managed to maintain itself with no migration. Instead, the family members depended on the eldest daughter, who worked in a pharmacy in Oaxaca City, and they farmed about 2 hectares of land locally. More typically, large families would include at least one migrant.

The above example points to the ways in which demography combines with other social indicators (landholdings, pooling of activities) to influence outcomes such as migration. In addition, although a family's size does not fully cause or inhibit migration, trends in growth and, in particular, large birth cohorts of the kind that are common from the 1950s to the present in rural Oaxaca can promote migration. According to Massey et al. (1998, 11), "[Rapid rises in population] put pressure on social infrastructure such as schools, roads, hospitals, and clinics; they make the satisfaction of consumer desires more difficult; they make it harder to provide decent and affordable housing; they raise unemployment rates; and generally they channel state resources away from productive investment into current consumption, driving up public expenditures and contributing to state deficits and foreign debts." For rural Oaxacans, this process—and in particular the combination of rising unemployment and declining wages—drives increasing migration rates.

Demography also works in more discrete and local ways to influence decision making among age cohorts over time (Keely 2000, 46). Headlines in the state's many daily papers—including *Noticias,* the largest circulating daily—have noted that rural communities throughout Oaxaca are in a state of collapse as young adults leave for international destinations. In fact, we discovered a slight aging among household heads, but only in communities with high rates of out-migration.

In San Juan Guelavia, household heads were older than one might expect. On average, the household heads were in their mid- to late fifties, whereas they were in their late thirties in the majority of 590 households surveyed. This shift appears to correlate with the rise of migration. Nevertheless, our survey found little overall change in the ages of household heads when we aggregated all households in our sample.

A second example reminds us that we cannot focus solely on migration and that following demographic trends can illuminate more than international processes. In San Martín Tilcajete, demography influenced outcomes for circuit moves, as well as for national and international migrations. Younger women and older men tended to commute to Oaxaca in search of work. At the same time, older women and younger men were more likely to travel to national destinations. Finally, very few women and mostly younger men made up the pool of San Martín's citizens who traveled to the United States for labor.

Returning to the question of household demographics I raised above, the number of minors that a household had to support had little bearing on migration. Instead, the overall size of a household (the total of members in the household) proved significant in migration outcomes. Migration rates do not necessarily increase as households cope with the arrival of more children; rather, as children age and gain some independence (and begin to demand goods, services, schooling, and wage labor of their own), it is likely that household members will migrate. Thus migration decisions are made in regard to a complex of issues, including the outcomes of the moves as anticipated by the individual mover, his or her age and gender, and a household's size.[9]

SOCIOECONOMIC PROCESSES AND MIGRATION

The importance of social networks in the decision to migrate has been discussed. We discovered that about 65% of all the migrants who left their central valley homes knew a migrant who lived at their destination. Migrant men relied a little less on these networks (62% used them), and migrant women a little more (68%). Migrants, particularly women, also followed friends and other members of their households to their destinations, and 60% of the women who migrated to the United States followed a brother or a father across the border.

Such linkages are profoundly important as individuals ponder the costs and benefits of migration, no matter if they plan to cross into the United States and seek work in Southern California or if they head to Baja California to find work in agricultural fields. However, other social and cultural forces are at work in the decision to migrate. There are the demands that children put on their parents for luxury goods—televisions, videocassette recorders, and compact disc players—that cannot be purchased with maize. If a household hopes to purchase a vehicle or to invest in stock animals, it must first find the money, and this is difficult when 80% of the households we surveyed make no more than twice the minimum wage (or about US$10 a day).

Migration may not be the easiest way to earn the money necessary to make the purchases that individuals want, but it is likely the most effective means available. In fact, in communities where more households earned more than twice the minimum wage, migration was lower. For example, in Guadalupe Etla and San Pablo Huitzo, 41% of the former's households and 45% of the latter's made well above the minimum wage. These communities also had a goodly number of households sending members to Oaxaca City for wage labor and salaried work, and only a little more than 20% of households were involved in international migration.

A second factor that influenced the decision to migrate related to language and ethnicity. Both San Juan del Río and Santa Inés Yatzeche are indigenous communities where Zapotec is spoken. We discovered that indigenous Oaxacans (defined by whether they speak an Indian language) are likely to choose migration to the United States over commuting and internal moves. We believe that this choice is due to the discrimination that indigenous peoples continue to suffer within Mexico. A Zapotec who commutes from Santa Inés Yatzeche to Oaxaca City is an Indian and therefore faces an uphill battle for respect vis-à-vis Oaxacan society. If, on the other hand, that Zapotec migrates to the United States, he or she becomes a Mexican as defined by the larger Anglo American community. The result is that one identity is traded for another, and new kinds of discrimination are encountered once the migrant is in the United States. Nevertheless, the opportunities that are present in the United States do not appear to be limited by the migrants' local or indigenous ethnicity, and the Zapotec becomes "another Mexican."

Third, communities whose populations are involved in migration are often described in the literature as coping with a migration syndrome, often described as "Norteñización" (see, for example, the discussion in Alarcón 1992 and Reichert 1981). The migration syndrome occurs when a community's citizens organize themselves around migration rather than around local economic and sociocultural processes (see Massey et al. 1998, 267). In other words, the urge to migrate and the loss of the local adult population to the pull of jobs and the promise of higher wages offset internal ties that maintain and reproduce households and communities. These losses are manifest in the comments made by older Oaxacans concerning the lack of respect that young Oaxacans show for traditional patterns of government, *tequio* and rituals support, and the *cargo* system. We heard complaints from nearly every *presidente municipal* whom we interviewed. However, there were few outward signs of a decline in participation among migrants. In fact, migrant households had levels of participation in *cargo* systems similar to those of their nonmigrant neighbors, and over time migrants tended to serve in more *cargos* and in higher-ranking positions in those *cargos* than nonmigrants did. Finally, many leaders depended upon the regular remittances of their children to cover the costs of their participation in community government.

An interview we had with a community leader in San Juan del Estado in June 2000 illustrates these points. The *presidente municipal* commented, "The young men in this town, they just want to do drugs, get high, and go to the United States. They don't want to work." However, in San Juan del Estado we found that the demand for positions was greater than the number of positions available locally, and community members continued to associate status and prestige with service.

Even with the increase in rates of migration and ease of movement, outcomes of migration and remittance use are not homogeneous. Rather, a range of outcomes can be found in any community (Massey et al. 1998, 27). In other words, some households will be relatively better off and migration will contribute to their success, while other households will suffer, even when migrants are present. The differences separating the better off from the worse off—or the relative deprivation of a given household in relation to the group (Stark and Taylor 1986; Stark and Yitzhaki 1988)—become themselves a motivating force in additional migration.

Three

CONTEMPORARY MIGRATION

Men really started leaving the community in 1945. Many people left, like my uncle—I haven't heard from him in years. Crossing was dangerous. . . . Me? No, I would never leave. I sell vegetables here in the village and in the Centro de Abastos [Oaxaca City's main daily market]. I can earn enough money to buy anything I need for my home and family.

JOSEFINA GUTIÉRREZ, SAN PEDRO IXTLAHUACA, JULY 2001

I met my husband when he came to Sinaloa eight years ago with his dad and older brother. We worked in the fields together. He is there now, living with my mother and working. I'm here and living with my girls and my mother-in-law. We've had this house for about one year. We don't have any land of our own, so she [my mother-in-law] helps me out. When I need help, his family comes. My husband works with his dad, and they will both be back to harvest his dad's land. . . . Yes, it is hard, but it is necessary. The money he sends is what I use to buy everything the family needs, my girls, my home, everything.

ALICIA HURTADO, SANTA MARÍA GUELACÉ, JUNE 2000

In 1994, the young men of this town left en masse.

ESPERANZA TORRES, GUADALUPE ETLA, JUNE 2001

I first went to the United States in 1994. I went solely for the support of my mother, my wife, and my children. We have work here; my mom makes cheese and sells milk to the cooperative. I have my land. But there were no sales to be made. I went to the United States for economic opportunities that I couldn't find here. So in 1994, I left. I sent money home every month. My wife was able to save what I sent, and she bought a ***yunta*** *[team of oxen]. Then she used some of the money to pay* ***cooperación*** *in the village. Some money went to the fiestas, and it is extremely important to help the pueblo, but the rest of the money we left in the bank. It is for our home, our family.*

ALFONSO TORRES (ESPERANZA'S SON), GUADALUPE ETLA, JUNE 2001

Why Oaxacans migrate is not an easy question to answer. Many factors influence the decision to migrate, including a household's size, the age of its heads, and its location in relation to Oaxaca City. Before we try to understand the variation in rural Oaxacan migration, it is useful first to have a basic idea of what a typical or average migrant looks like.

Oaxacan migrants are most likely men crossing into the United States (see table 2.1). In fact, 65% of all migrations from the central valleys are destined for the United States. The majority of the migrants moving to the United States are male (66%), female migrants to the United States are a much smaller group (17%), and the gender of the remaining migrants is unknown.

Although Oaxacan men were most likely to cross the U.S. border as migrants, and even though U.S.-bound migration dominates discussions of migration, we cannot ignore those migrants who were bound for internal destinations, nor should we disregard the moves of migrant women. We found that 35% of all moves made by central valley migrants were to internal destinations. Thus, although our typical mover was a young man, there was a substantial group of Oaxacan women who migrated as well. Furthermore, internal migration was more evenly divided between the genders. Forty percent of internal migrants were men, and 38% were women.

With these caveats concerning the structure of the migrant population, we can define a "typical" Oaxacan migrant. The typical Oaxacan migrant is a married man in his mid-twenties. His wife is about two years younger than him on average. Together the couple manages a nuclear household that includes two or three minors (accounting for 63% of households). The couple and their children usually live adjacent to the male head's siblings, parents, or sometimes both (all organized around nuclear family units). Although the various nuclear units are largely independent, they rely upon each other for temporary support when necessary, whether that means feeding and caring for young children, aiding in farmwork, or participating in community government.

There is a significant but small correlation between the size of a household and the number of migrants that the household will include. Smaller household units (with four or fewer members) do not typically include more than one migrant, no matter the age of the minors in that household. Migrant households with four or more members typically have at least two migrating members and can have more.

The relationship of household size to migration is not linear. Rather, migration rates plot following a curve, rising to two migrants per household when there are between four and six members, rising slightly higher with more members, and then declining to zero as the members in the household increase to more than eight in total. Thus having children, though not necessarily a bad strategy for a household hoping to increase the number of workers it can deploy, does bring some risks, not the least of which is having to care for and feed extra members during their growth and development. Further, the burden of additional nonworking members may make migration an option that is too costly to undertake. Additionally, children do not necessarily support their households when they are adults, and approximately 25% of the migrant households we contacted reported that their migrating members were in contact with their sending households but were not remitting.

Households combine labor and effort to support themselves over time and space (Netting et al. 1984). The male head farms about 1.5 hectares of land, and he harvests enough maize to feed his family for a little more than six months. He supplements farmwork with limited wage labor when possible. This typically means that he finds work on construction sites throughout the valleys and can often earn twice the daily minimum wage, or about US$10 per day, for his time and effort.

The female head of the household combines nonwage domestic work in the household with moneymaking activities that supplement the household's budget. She earns money through the sale of prepared foods such as tortillas or in some cases through the sale of harvested vegetables and dairy products. She earns additional income by taking work into the home, usually laundry and ironing.

Older and adult children supplement the household's budget by turning their wages over to a parent or participating in work around the home (craft production, farming, and so forth) that indirectly contributes to income generation. For the 35% of households that follow a more extended, multigenerational model (about 60% of the extended households consisted of five to eight members), there are additional members who can migrate, participate in wage earning, and assist in maintenance and household management.

A rural Oaxacan decides to migrate because he wants first to feed and maintain his family and to outfit his home with modern conveniences and small appliances and perhaps later to help his children enter postprimary educational programs. If his wife can manage to cover most of the household's expenses, the couple will earmark some remittances for building, renovating, or expanding their home—adding a modern bathroom, a second floor, and a modern kitchen complete with running water, a refrigerator, and a gas stove.

A rural Oaxacan migrant chooses between a national and an international destination based upon the relationships he holds with already settled migrants or the networks he establishes through family and friends. Just over half of the time, he travels to a U.S. destination where the majority of migrants are headed. In the United States, he will settle in Southern California, around the Los Angeles–Santa Monica area.

About 35% of central valley migrants have traveled to national destinations such as Mexico City, Tapachula, Chiapas, or the agricultural fields of Baja California at some point in their career. Of this total, slightly more than half are from households that also have members with migration experience in the United States. Internal movers in the present day are bound for the D.F. (Mexico City), border cities such as Ciudad Juárez, or Baja California. Tapachula, Chiapas, attracted migrants during the 1980s and early 1990s when the city's economy boomed, but that movement has slowed in recent years.

Migrants to the D.F. tend to find work as domestics (particularly women), in service, or in construction (predominantly men). Migrants bound for border cities typically plan to continue across the border and into the United States, but for one reason or another cannot make the cross. For some there is a lack of funds or connections, others find work on the Mexican side of the border, and we heard of two migrants from San Juan del Estado who decided to come home after unnerving experiences at the border. Like their international counterparts, internal migrants settle with family or friends, although some single women live in the households of their employers (see Howell 1999; Rees and Coronel Ortiz 2002).

About 7% of the migrants we interviewed reported migrating first to a national destination and later to an international destination. These movers often had family and friends settled in both the United States and other parts of Mexico and thus had access to support networks in each of their destination communities. Some of these migrants began their sojourns with internal migrations, and only after some success did they move on to cross the border. Nevertheless, movers who began in Mexico and ended in the United States benefited from the cumulative histories of migration in their households and communities (Massey 1990).

Local circuit moves and daily commutes between villages and regional centers remain important for men and women in the central valley. Overall, 38% of rural central valley households send at least one person to Oaxaca City for work. However, 39% of households with migrants bound for national destinations also have members working in the city. For households with migrants bound for the U.S. border, 25% also have members that work in Oaxaca City. Finally, 41% of the households with migrants in both U.S. and national destinations include commuters traveling to Oaxaca City for work. Thus, migration is not an either-or process. A migrant does not decide independently that he or she will travel to Mexico or the United States; rather the decision is dynamic; reflects a household's needs, size, and status; and can include multiple destinations.

Once a migrant has decided upon a destination, he or she must organize the money necessary to cover the expenses of migration (table 3.1). Travel to the United States can cost thousands of dollars. Migrants need money to cover their transportation and the fees and bribes they need to pay to smugglers and officials. There can be a lag between when migrants arrive in the United States and when they find work, so they also need money to cover expenses upon arrival.

Most migrants (91%) from the central valleys meet these expenses by spending their own savings or using money that a friend or family member has given to them as a gift or a loan. Other migrants use savings from their families, and these migrants usually remit directly to a parent rather than to their spouse. A small group funds their sojourns through loans (4%). Most loans come from a member of a family or from an older member of the community who is typically described as a jefe (boss).

A jefe in this sense is a mentor, a person who is often a compadre of the migrant and who may have taught the migrant many of the skills he or she will use in life. In craft-producing communities, a jefe is usually the person who taught young individuals their craft. A jefe may also provide a future migrant with petty jobs around the jefe's homestead. In any case, a jefe is not a loan shark, and loans made by a jefe do not come with exorbitant interest rates. A commercially secured loan (from an individual who is usually described as a loan shark) can bear extremely high interest (as much as 10% monthly); only one of the loans reported in our surveys was secured

TABLE 3.1 MEETING THE COSTS OF MIGRATION TO THE UNITED STATES

Source of funds	*No. of migrants using funding source*[a]
Personal savings	58 (42%)
Family money	54 (39%)
Gifts from friends/family	14 (10%)
Loans	6 (4%)
Sale of animals	4 (3%)
Other	2 (1%)
Total	138

[a] Total does not add up to 100% because of rounding

at a commercial office. We did not encounter individuals who admitted to signing a contract with an employer who would cover the costs of reaching the United States in exchange for labor.

Knowing someone at the destination was critical for many migrants. Sixty percent of the migrants interviewed followed a relative or friend to the United States and depended on that person for support. Among migrants with international destinations, women were slightly more likely to depend upon these connections than men, whereas men showed a slightly higher dependence on these connections for internal migrations. Migrant women also were much more likely to follow a family member (usually a father or a brother) to their destination. We found that 60% of all the women who migrated to the United States came from a household that had already sent a male member across the border. On the other hand, only 17% of the men came from households with female migrants established in the United States.

Repeatedly informants told us that a critical factor in their decision making, one they were convinced would lead to their success as a migrant, was to be related to a migrant who had already succeeded. A tie to a successful migrant in a destination community leads to jobs, a place to live, and a network of support (see Massey 1990). These relationships are also critical when the migrant is considered unwelcome by the local Anglo-American majority in his or her destination community (Zlolniski 2001).

The majority of migrants traveling to internal destinations settled with family, and those traveling to the United States settled with family or friends (86% of the total number of international movers) once they had

TABLE 3.2 DESTINATIONS FOR INTERNAL AND U.S.-BOUND MIGRANTS

Destination	*Number of migrants*
Internal migrants	
Communities in Oaxaca	6
Distrito Federal (Mexico City)	44
Baja California	14
Nuevo León	4
Other state in Mexico	10
Total	78
U.S.-bound migrants	
California	133
Other	9
Total	142

reached their destination. Family included other members of a household, cousins, and siblings; in one case a migrant settled with his grandparents in Mexico City. Only one U.S.-bound migrant lived with his employer on a farm in California.

More internal migrants (16%) lived with their employers. In this case, seven of the nine migrants (all female) who reported living with an employer were domestics or servants in households. Of the two remaining, one was a male employed as a groundskeeper at a plant in Mexico City, and the other, a fifty-four-year-old woman, did not describe her employment. Migrants who lived with family or friends in the United States were typically found in apartment complexes that housed other migrants from the same hometown or region of the state.

Migrants destined for the United States typically settle in Southern California, with the majority of migrants (54%) moving into the Los Angeles–Santa Monica area (table 3.2). A very small number of migrants move to new destinations. The nine migrants who were not in California had settled in Oregon, Texas, New Jersey, New York, Virginia, Illinois, and Pennsylvania, but seven of the nine began their sojourns in Southern California. Internal migrants settled primarily in the Distrito Federal (Mexico City), with a smaller population moving to Baja California.

Both internal and international migrants from the central valleys found similar kinds of employment once they had settled in their receiving communities (table 3.3). The service sector (restaurants, hotels, gas stations, and convenience stores) employed more rural Oaxacans living in the United States than any other job sector (48%). Wage work (construction and unskilled labor positions) employed 14% of the migrant pool. Agricultural work (farm labor) perhaps somewhat surprisingly, given our image of the Mexican migrant, employed only 16% of rural Oaxacans. However, agricultural labor is something that most Oaxacans described as difficult, dirty work that was not worth the trouble of migration. An additional 13% of Oaxacans were employed as gardeners for private households and small landscaping firms. Just 8% of Oaxacans in the United States are employed as domestic workers.

Only 4% of the Oaxacans with migration experience in the United States described a job that was atypical. For example, one young woman was employed as an assistant in a private kindergarten; an older man organized a small *tienda* in his apartment complex; and a third migrant, a young Oaxacan woman, was employed in a hospital as a nurse and held a green card. Only one U.S. migrant described his position as a professional one—he worked as a manager for a small construction firm in San Diego, California. He too held a green card and moved freely across the border.

Internal migrants were also employed in the service sector (29%). A small percentage of internal migrants also found work in agriculture (7%), settling in Baja California. More internal migrants were employed as domestics (30%), and a little more than a quarter of these positions were "live-in" jobs. One important difference between internal and international migrants was the higher number of professionals found within the

TABLE 3.3 EMPLOYMENT FOR INTERNAL AND U.S.-BOUND MIGRANTS

Employment	*Number of internal migrants*	*Number of U.S.-bound migrants*
Service work	16	61
Unspecified wage work	10	18
Domestic work	17	8
Agricultural work	4	20
Gardeners	0	16
Professional work	4	1
Other	5	4
Total	56	128

country. The number of professional migrants moving internally is quite small (4 of 56 migrants), but a higher percentage than we found among international movers (7% of national movers versus less than 1% of international migrants).[1] This is not a significant difference, but it does indicate that a combination of limited educational opportunities and the undocumented status of most Oaxacan migrants in the United States narrows their available job opportunities. Professionals identified in our surveys included a surgeon, a politician, an accountant, and an owner-manager of several restaurants. In the "other" category were two photographers (brothers), a teacher, and two trained technicians who worked for large businesses.

There is a great deal of variation in the total time that migrants spend away from their hometown households. Short-term sojourns were obvious, lasting a minimum of six months away from home. Some of the migrants who made short-term sojourns described their experience as very negative; others had not found work, and they returned home to reduce the rising costs of their sojourns. Santiago García, a twenty-six-year-old from San Juan del Estado who had spent only six months in the United States, complained, "I just didn't like the United States. I missed home and my kids, and I couldn't find a job." Other short-term stays were reported by household heads and concerned recent migrants new to their destination community. These individuals had not yet experienced more than a year or two of life as a migrant.

Maximum lengths of stay varied greatly for individuals and for households. U.S.-bound migrants spent on average just a little less than nine years in the United States. Nevertheless, the median for U.S.-bound migrants was five years, and 35% of all migrants spent no more than two years in the United States.

Generally, households sent one member to the United States as a migrant, and only about 8% of households sent more than two migrants. For households with more than one migrant, we totaled the years each migrant spent in the United States. Using this figure, we discovered that some migrant households had extremely high totals of years spent in the United States. For example, seven households included migrants who collectively had spent well over twenty-five years working in the United States.

Typical was the Sánchez Méndez household in San Juan Guelavia. The household's three sons and one daughter had collectively spent about forty-five years in the United States. In 1975, Roberto (then nineteen years of age) migrated to the United States to take a job in Pasadena, following a tip from a relative who had spent time in the United States. Roberto worked for the next twenty years at a series of agricultural and service jobs in Southern California. He lived with relatives and returned to San Juan Guelavia when he could, marrying a young woman from the village in 1980. He encouraged his younger siblings to join him in the United States, and in 1980 a second brother crossed the border. In 1985 a third brother crossed, and finally in 1990 his younger sister crossed into the United States.

Internal migration followed a pattern similar to that for international moves. Internal migrations varied in length. They averaged eleven years, but the median was only six years. Just over 30% of all internal movers spent no more than three years away from home, and only 20% spent sixteen or more years away from home.

Households with internal movers typically had only one migrant, and only 7.5% of households had more than three migrants. However, a few households had many migrants and migrants who made repeated moves within national boundaries.

Except for households whose members migrate en masse, a household must continue to maintain itself during a migrant's absence. This can be difficult and can challenge the organizational skills, patience, and abilities of those left at home. The dilemma of migration became evident to me when I had opportunities in 1996 and 2000 to interview several women who were supporting households in Santa Ana del Valle, Guadalupe Etla, Santa María Guelacé, and San Juan del Estado while their husbands worked in the United States.

Anita Sánchez described her situation in Santa Ana during the three years (1996 to 1999) that her husband, Alfonso Martinez, worked construction in San Diego, California. Anita and her two children, Gordo and Isabel (ages two and six at the time), moved into her parents' home, where they stayed for nearly the entire period that Alfonso was away. She described her situation and living at home as "less than optimal," but the alternatives—living alone with no income or living with her mother-in-law—were not viable options. She also noted that if she had remained at home, the money her husband returned would have gone to feeding her and the children, not to purchase materials to improve the home. As it was, a good portion of the remittances she received went to cover living expenses, school-related fees, and community expenses.

Returning to her parents' home reduced the pressure on her to use remittances for household maintenance, and she had built-in child care for her children that allowed her to weave with her father part-time. However, her decision to live with her parents and not her mother-in-law angered her husband. He wanted her to stay with his mother or in their new home. He described her return to her parents' home as a humiliating moment for him. He said, "I worked really hard to care for her and Gordo and Isabel. I built this house for them. When they left, it really hurt. I spent so much time working, I was gone for so long, but she wouldn't stay by my side—she just ran home." Luckily, the situation moderated by 2001, and when I returned to talk with the couple again, they had worked out their differences. They lived in a new two-story home (built with remittances), they had a third child, and Alfonso was filling a position in a minor *cargo* for the community. Nevertheless, this story also suggests that even as migration is integrated into local society, there are moments when traditional systems of support fail. In this case, Alfonso's decision to migrate did not work out as planned and created additional stress in the family.

A quite different quality is apparent in the stories I heard from two sisters in Guadalupe Etla. They had married two brothers who, at nearly sixty years of age, continued to live and work in Mexico City. The brothers had originally migrated to Mexico City in the 1960s to pursue higher education. They received technical training, secured union work, and brought their young wives to live with them. Over the course of the next forty years, they moved back and forth between Guadalupe Etla and Mexico City. As their children were born, the sisters returned off and on to Guadalupe Etla. In 1990 the sisters returned to Guadalupe Etla permanently, and their husbands remained in Mexico City.

The sisters were quite animated and amusing as they described their current situation as optimal. "Look at our lovely house! We have our small store [a *tienda* that sells sundries and school supplies near one of the community's schools], three of my children live here, and my grandchildren live here. I am quite happy to be rid of Mexico City and its noise and bother." "Nevertheless," I asked, "don't you miss your husband?" Señora Rosaria laughed for a moment and replied, "Do I miss him? Not at all. He isn't here to bother me, I don't have to cook for him or clean for him, I don't pick up after him, and he isn't here to wear me out! [*Winks.*]"

A poignant story came from Señora Josefina in Santa María Guelacé. Her husband had left for the United States in 1998 and had slowly remitted money to her following more or less a bimonthly schedule. Generally, she could anticipate about US$300 from her husband every other month. However, they earmarked the money to cover the costs of building a new home so that Josefina, her husband, and their daughter (age four) could move out of the home of Josefina's mother-in-law. Josefina and her mother-in-law (María) worked together as *tortilleras.* The work was hard. They woke early to get to the mill, grind the maize, and start the fire for cooking. In a small cane structure they spent several hours in the smoke and soot, baking tortillas. Three days a week Josefina hauled several kilos of tortillas to Oaxaca City, where she sold them in the northeast zonal market. María stayed home with her granddaughter. Josefina and María earned about 500 pesos (US$50) a week and were able to cover most of their expenses. María also supplemented their budget by taking in laundry on occasion. Josefina used the remittances her husband sent to purchase building supplies in anticipation of his return and hoped that their household would remain free of any sudden disaster or crisis. Although the situation worked well on paper, it was very stressful for Josefina, as well as María. Josefina does not get along well with her mother-in-law, and because she married into the community, she has no other family in the area. Her exhaustion is evident as she cooks a meal for her daughter, cleans up for the day, and plans for making tortillas in the morning.

A final example comes from San Juan del Estado. Señora Alicia Cruz had sent her husband to the United States in 1999, only about a half a year before we interviewed her. She described the situation as manageable. She had three older children, and they helped her with the household. Together they maintained six dairy cows and produced enough cheese to sell some locally. She also rented 2 hectares of land *por la mitad*. The land was irrigated and of a good quality. The harvest was expected to provide the household with nearly a year's worth of maize. Alicia's younger children attended school, and Alicia hoped to send at least one to Oaxaca City for postsecondary education.

Each of the households described above continued to pool resources and relied upon cooperation to survive. Coping with migration was an exercise that the members hoped would maintain and ideally improve their households. Nevertheless, the situation was never an easy one to manage. A migrant's remittances often arrive intermittently and amounts fluctuate from month to month. Husbands who are away from their hometowns grow lonely, tired, and angry when they think about their families and children left behind. Wives grow angry as well, for they are burdened with the full support of their children and must balance the demands of the household against the fear that their husband may think they were wasteful during his sojourn. Some households lose members to accidents, and others have members who disappear. In Guadalupe Etla an elderly woman began to sob as she described how her daughter simply vanished one day several years ago, never to be heard from again. Marriages that take place in the United States or other parts of Mexico can also complicate matters.

Señora Esperanza Villalobos, fifty-three years old, lived in San Juan del Río and told us about her two younger brothers. Both had left the village years earlier for New York; she was not sure of which community they lived in or if they lived in the city. For several years, they had remitted to her parents. Both were now married to U.S.-born women, and both resided full-time in the United States with their families. Although they visit the community from time to time, they no longer send remittances, because they are busy supporting their own families now.

A household with migrants who have left is not free of its social obligations and must meet its responsibilities, such as participating in *tequio, cooperación,* and *servicio.* Some households hire replacements to cover their *tequio* and *servicio.* However, the percentages of such households remain small. Only about 12% of the household heads we interviewed said they had hired a replacement to cover their *tequio,* and less than 1% hired a replacement to fulfill a member's election to a *cargo* or a *comite.* A relative who is asked to take the place of the missing migrant typically fills the gap in *servicio.* Fathers regularly serve for their sons, but this is not always a smooth process. Don Julio, an elderly man in Santa Ana del Valle, spent four consecutive years filling positions for his sons who were in the United States. The work was not hard, but Don Julio had retired from service after many years spent filling *cargos* for his household and did not look forward to filling his sons' positions. In addition, financial support from migrants living away from their hometowns, though critical to a community (see Smith 1998), is not equivalent to spending time in a *cargo* or giving *tequio.*

Women are now moving into *cargo* and *comite* positions throughout the valleys. In the past, *servicio* was something that occupied men's time and energy and the resources of their households. Men publicly created their status through this process. Although the status they earned for their work generalized to their household, the work itself was traditionally limited only to men. As the number of *comites* expanded and the people to fill them migrated, there was increasing pressure to fill the growing list of positions. In general, population growth kept up with demand, and there were enough men to fill positions as they came open. Furthermore, as Frank Cancian (1965) demonstrated in his pathbreaking work in Zinacantán, Chiapas, there was great competition among men at least for high-status posts; and one way to move on to high-status posts was to fill lower-status positions successfully.

Competition for prestige continues to drive *cargo* and *comite* participation in most rural Oaxacan communities. Party-based politics have yet to penetrate the Oaxacan countryside, and participation in *cargos* remains high. A majority of central valley households (65%) included members who were currently in a *cargo* or *comite* position. Only 2% of households reported that members had never served in the *cargo* system, while 6% had completed their service and were retired. An additional 8% were "resting" or between positions. The remaining households (19%) would not comment on their participation.

Even with the continued importance of the *cargos* and *comites,* migration does draw men away from their commitments to their communities. A relatively new solution finds the wives of migrants filling the positions to which their husbands were elected. Women's participation in the system began not with migration but with the formation of a series of relatively low-status *comites* around family-based programs, including LICONSA (Leche Industrializada Conasupo, often referred to as the *leche comite* because it distributes subsidized milk to families); craft cooperatives; and educational programs. The experience of women in these *comites* and programs served them well as they began to show up in place of their husbands.

Gloria Martínez, a young mother in Villa Díaz Ordaz, described what happened in January 1998 when she showed up for a meeting of the *comite del agua potable* in place of her husband, Juan, who had been elected to the position of *vocal* (voting member) even though he had recently left for the United States:

> I went to that first meeting, and oh my, was it ever quiet! Everyone was looking at me. I just told them, 'You don't want me here? Well, fine! I've got my kids to take care of—I'm happy to go home. But I'm happy to work too, so stop staring at me!' That quieted them down, but they were really mad about it—they were really mad at Juan. They were mostly mad that I wouldn't let them drink. I said, 'Look, I've got my kids to feed. I don't want to waste my time.' And I think they were too embarrassed to drink in front of me anyway. Finally they let me stay, and I think we got good work done. We probably got more done because I was there and the other members were so nervous! *[Laughs.]*
>
> GLORIA MARTÍNEZ, VILLA DÍAZ ORDAZ, MAY 2000

Later I had an opportunity to talk to another member of the *comite del agua potable.* He did in fact say that Gloria was a surprise and that the *comite*'s members were angry that Juan was not serving in the position to which he had been elected. He grumbled about Gloria's presence and that she kept the entire *comite* much more serious. However, he also admitted that the

Women in the LICONSA comite, *Santa Ana del Valle. Author photo.*

comite probably worked harder and accomplished more because of Gloria's presence.

We found that women held minor positions in nearly every community we visited. In many cases women filled *comite* slots to which their husbands had been nominated, but in Santa Inés Yatzeche and Guadalupe Etla, we met young women who had been elected to fill the position of municipal secretary. Their election reflected their educational status and literacy. The changes in the *comites* were dramatic and profound and had taken place quickly. In 1992, I watched community elections held over two days in Santa Ana del Valle. During a lull in the nomination process, a point at which no men would stand for election, the director of the election process threatened to open the floor and nominate women. The crowd protested and laughed, and in any case no women were present. Less then ten years later, women were filling positions and being named for service.

Finally, we also found that in addition to the *cargo* systems, *cooperación* remains critically important to these communities. Ninety-eight percent of households reported making regular contributions to community programs and projects. These contributions ranged from 50 pesos (about US$5) to support school programs and road repairs to 500 pesos that some households contributed toward fiestas and rituals.

In addition to the outcomes that the decision to migrate has for Oaxacans from the central valleys, we also studied the variations in migration outcomes among central valley communities. Differences in migration outcomes were quite profound among the communities (table 3.4). An average of about 47% of any community's households were involved in migration. However, when we looked at specific communities, we found that rates of migration (that is, the percentage of households that have migrant members) varied greatly, as did the destinations migrants chose. San Pablo Huitzo had the lowest rate of migration of the communities surveyed; 22% of its households had migrant members. At the other end of the scale, 62% of the households in San Juan Guelavia included migrants.

To capture the diversity of movement, I designed a correspondence analysis with the aid of Garry Chick, an anthropologist in Pennsylvania State University's program in leisure studies. The correspondence analysis plots the relationships among eleven communities, the four types of moves made by rural Oaxacans, and the communities and those movements.[2] (Because we lacked comparable data on movement for Santa Ana, it is not a part of this analysis.)

TABLE 3.4 MIGRATION OUTCOMES BY COMMUNITY

Community	*Households surveyed*	*Nonmigrant households*	*Commuter households*	*Internal migrant households*	*U.S. migrant households*
Guadalupe Etla	66	24	12	12	27
Santa Inés Yatzeche	30	12	1	1	16
Santa María Guelacé	28	11	5	7	5
San Juan del Estado	66	17	14	11	24
San Juan Guelavia	87	23	10	10	44
San Juan del Río	47	26	1	2	18
San Lorenzo Albarradas	56	35	4	8	9
San Martín Tilcajete	58	26	2	5	25
San Pablo Huitzo	41	18	14	3	6
San Pedro Ixtlahuaca	50	14	10	8	18
Villa Díaz Ordaz	61	31	5	9	16
Total	590	237	78	76	199

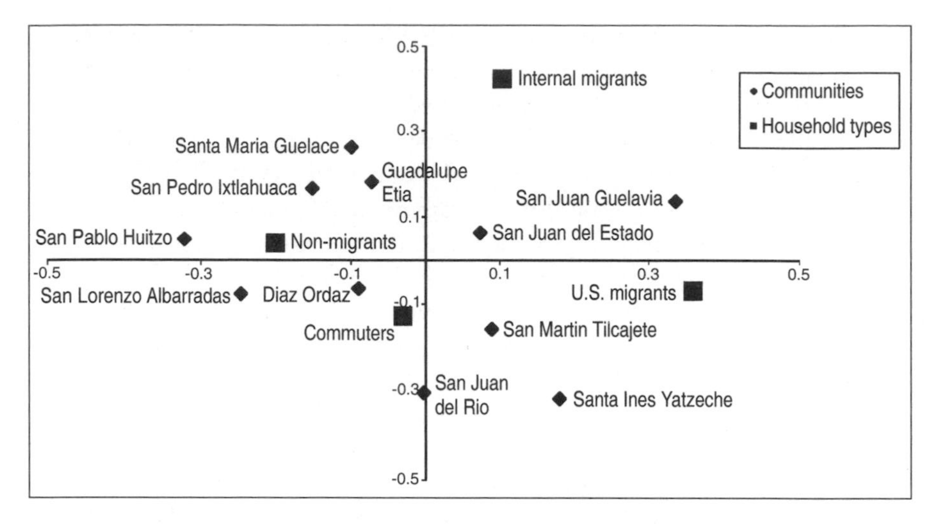

FIGURE 3.1. *Correspondence analysis. (Garry Chick conducted this analysis for an article in the journal* Field Methods; *see Cohen et al. 2003.)*

The correspondence analysis plots eleven communities and four outcomes (nonmigration, circuit moves, internal migration, and international migration) in relation to one another along *x*- and *y*-axes. The numerical values of the axes have no significance. Rather, the placement of migration outcomes and communities on the plot captures their relationships and associations. Communities that plot closer together are more similar (they correspond); communities that plot farther apart are more different (Weller and Romney 1990). In other words, communities that share similar migration rates and outcomes—for example, Santa María Guelacé and Guadalupe Etla—plot close together. Communities with quite different migration rates—for example, San Pablo Huitzo, where migration rates are low, and San Juan Guelavia, where migration rates are high—plot far apart. Similar outcomes also are plotted more closely than different outcomes. Internal and U.S.-bound migrations plot to the right of the *y*-axis, and nonmigrants and commuters plot to the left of the axis.

The four quadrants of the graph capture the particular outcomes or decisions that central valley households make concerning migration. Nonmigrant households plot in the upper left quadrant, and commuter households in the lower left quadrant. Internally bound migrants (those moving within national borders) are plotted in the upper right quadrant, and international migrants (those bound for the United States) plot in the lower right quadrant.

Communities plot on the graph in relation to each other and to migration decision outcomes. Communities that plot closer to the point where the outcomes intersect—San Juan del Estado, for example—show a more generalized pattern of migration outcomes. In other words, the communities toward the center of the plot exhibit a diversity of outcomes and have similar-sized groups of nonmigrants, circuit movers, internal migrants, and international movers.

Communities that plot farther from the center of the graph show less variation in migration outcomes for member households. Households in San Pablo Huitzo, for example, do not migrate at the levels found in other communities; furthermore, the community does not include a large group of circuit movers. Thus San Pablo Huitzo plots to the left of the nonmigrant point on the graph and relatively far from any of the other outcomes.

A community's relative placement in relation to the four outcomes is one indication of the importance of migration for that community's households. San Lorenzo Albarradas, a community where 63% of households do not participate in migration, plots in the nonmigrant quadrant. On the other hand, San Juan Guelavia, a community where 62% of households are involved in internal or international migration, plots to the right of the *y*-axis and between the internal and U.S.-bound migration quadrants, somewhat closer to the reference point for U.S.-bound migration. San Martín Tilcajete, a community with nearly identical populations of nonmigrant (45%) and U.S.-bound migrant households (43%), plots between the reference points for nonmigrants and U.S.-bound migrant households.

The correspondence analysis tells us where a community plots in relation to a set of potential outcomes, from nonmigration to U.S.-bound migration. We need to return to ethnographic and historical data to understand why a community plots where it does.

San Pablo Huitzo is an outlier along the *x*-axis, to the left of the reference point for nonmigrant households. However, San Pablo Huitzo is not a community with an uncharacteristically low rate of migration. In fact, San Pablo has a rich and complex history of migration that is rooted in the 1940s, when many households sent members to Mexico City.[3] This movement was facilitated first by the main rail line that passed through the community and connected Oaxaca to Puebla and Mexico City, and later by the arrival of the Pan-American Highway, which passes through village lands. Today Huitzeños maintain an enclave in Mexico City, and many return annually to their home village during saints' day celebrations. Before bus service was modernized (i.e., through the 1980s, according to informants), Huitzeños in Mexico City hired a priest and rented several train cars to take them and their children to Huitzo to celebrate the community's *patrón*. Now Huitzeños rent buses to make the journey.

A second factor that has limited local movements is Huitzo's role as a small magnet city for the area. Although there is regular bus service to Oaxaca City throughout the day, the community is home to a growing and diverse market economy that attracts locals from the region. But Huitzo lacks any centers for advanced training or education; thus students who want to pursue postsecondary education must travel to Oaxaca City.

San Lorenzo Albarradas is also positioned to the left of the nonmigrant reference point in the correspondence analysis, because nearly 63% of the community's households elect not to migrate. Of the remaining households, 7% follow local circuits to work and schools in the region, 14% leave for internal destinations, and 16% travel to the United States.

Unlike San Pablo Huitzo, San Lorenzo Albarradas lacks a long history of movement and has a limited local market economy. Additionally, although San Lorenzo is linked by road and bus service to area cities (most notably the market and political centers of Mitla and Tlacolula), it is an isolated settlement. Leaving the community is more difficult than it might be in communities with better access to regional centers and the capital city, and thus we find few of San Lorenzo's citizens following local circuits. Furthermore, because migration is relatively new to the area (the first migrant did not leave until 1970, and the bulk of migrants left after 1985), migration has not yet entered a phase where its benefits outweigh its costs (Massey et al. 1994). Finally, San Lorenzo Albarradas is an extremely marginal community, as defined by DIGEPO; it lacks adequate services, educational attainment is low, and laborers earn extremely low wages for their work. In fact, 100% of the households we surveyed did some farming every year, and just under half of all households produced crafts (typically *petates,* woven reed mats used for sleeping).

Santa Inés Yatzeche plots along the lower arm of the *y*-axis, in the U.S.-bound migrant quadrant. Like San Lorenzo Albarradas, Santa Inés Yatzeche is relatively far from Oaxaca City, and its access to the city is limited. Businesses in Zaachila, a regional center that borders Santa Inés Yatzeche, serve the needs of the community, but few of Santa Inés Yatzeche's citizens travel there for labor. Similarly, San Juan del Río is an isolated community that plots low on the *y*-axis and includes many nonmigrant households (55% of the total).

The distance of a community from Oaxaca City negatively correlates with circuit moves. In other words, members of households in communities that are farther from Oaxaca City are less likely to follow local circuits

A typical home in Santa Inés Yatzeche. Author photo.

to the city for work. On the other hand, there is a positive correlation between distance and U.S.-bound migration: households are more likely to send migrants to the United States when they are located at a greater distance from the state's capital. Additionally, although each community is linked by bus service to Oaxaca City, that service is not direct. In each case, commuters traveling to Oaxaca City must switch buses at least once. From San Lorenzo Albarradas and San Juan del Río, commuters must travel first to Mitla or Tlacolula and transfer (paying a second fare) to continue on to Oaxaca. Passengers originating in Santa Inés Yatzeche transfer in Zimatlán, and those traveling from Villa Díaz Ordaz transfer in Tlacolula. The transfers add both time and money to the commutes. Because the costs of circuit moves are high (as is the time needed to make those moves), households in these communities are more apt to consider migration. In the case of San Juan del Río and Santa Inés Yatzeche, those households that do elect to migrate typically choose a destination in the United States and do not invest their time or effort in circuit moves to Oaxaca City.

Several communities in the survey are also known for crafts of one kind or another. In some cases, craft production is a lucrative activity. However, craft production generally does not lead to economic growth. Rather a household can use it to "make do," and that is what we find in two outlier communities—San Juan del Río and San Lorenzo Albarradas—and to a much smaller degree in Villa Díaz Ordaz.

Mescal (an alcoholic beverage produced from agave plants) and *petates* are produced in San Juan del Río. Fifteen percent of the households we visited produced at least some mescal throughout the year, 43% produced *petates,* and 4% produced both. In San Lorenzo Albarradas, 45% of local households included artisans who produced *petates* and some cotton textiles. Most of the mescal produced in San Juan del Río is sold for local consumption, as are most of the *petates* made in both communities. The market for mescal was steady in San Juan, and much of the community's product was sold to bottlers in Santiago Matatlán. Nevertheless, the community was not directly tied to the boom in mescal in Oaxaca City—mainly because producers in the town were too far from the city to cash in on the mescal craze. Tourists who traveled to the coast purchased *petates* for the beach, but again, sales were very low. Thus neither craft nor mescal had much effect on the status of local households or on migration outcomes.

The situation was somewhat different in Villa Díaz Ordaz, where only 11% of the community's households were involved in craft production. In Villa Díaz Ordaz, artisans produced woolen textiles as part of a large complex of weaving villages whose economy was centered in Teotitlán del Valle (Stephen 1991). Production followed a "putting out" model in Villa Díaz Ordaz, with the majority of textiles going directly to middlemen in Teotitlán del Valle and few sales made locally (see Cohen 1998). The *presidente municipal* of the community believed that the control that Teotitlán del Valle exerted over the production of woolen textiles was effectively forcing most Ordázeans out of the market.

A variable that proved to have a significant impact on the decision to make circuit moves for Santa Inés Yatzeche, San Juan del Río, Villa Díaz Ordaz, and San Juan Guelavia was ethnicity, or, more to the point, the presence of Zapotec or Chinantec speakers (table 3.5). Speaking a native language negatively correlated with circuit moves. In other words, Zapotec and Chinantec speakers were less likely to follow circuits to Oaxaca

TABLE 3.5 INDIGENOUS POPULATIONS BY COMMUNITY

Community	*Indigenous population (%)*
Guadalupe Etla	6.29
San Juan del Estado	0.54
San Juan del Río	98.13
San Juan Guelavia	89.30
San Lorenzo Albarradas	19.61
San Martín Tilcajete	0.84
San Pablo Huitzo	3.65
San Pedro Ixtlahuaca	0.98
Santa Ana del Valle	94.70
Santa Inés Yatzeche	99.74
Santa María Guelacé	39.36
Villa Díaz Ordaz	92.42

City and other regional centers than were Spanish speakers. Nevertheless, speaking an indigenous language had no correlation with internal or international migrations. This suggests that an indigenous identity (defined through language) carried a stigma in the state, and that stigma affected an individual's ability to succeed in Oaxaca.

Indigenous Oaxacans often chose instead to migrate out of the state or to the United States as a way to escape local prejudice. In other parts of Mexico, native speakers from Oaxaca were able to blend in with local peasant populations in an effort to find-better paying wages. In the United States, native Oaxacans became "Mexican" and could generally join the undocumented community and lose their indigenous identity.

San Pedro Ixtlahuaca, Santa María Guelacé, and Guadalupe Etla cluster in the nonmigrant quadrant of the correspondence analysis. These communities are relatively closer to Oaxaca City than other villages surveyed, and they share a plethora of transportation possibilities for accessing the city—direct bus service, taxi service, and *collectivos* (taxis that follow set routes between hometowns and Oaxaca City). Nevertheless, more than location and access to the city explains why these communities cluster in the analysis.

Work was a critical factor in the importance of circuit moves to these communities. Farmers in Santa María Guelacé used their location near the city to gain ready and quick access to zonal markets and restaurants for their produce, most notably garlic grown in the village (and 96% of the community's households farmed). Similarly, dairy producers in Guadalupe Etla supplied area markets with milk and cheese and tended not to migrate with the frequency of typical households in the area.

Women from San Pedro Ixtlahuaca accessed a different market. Many of these women had traveled to Oaxaca City to sell tortillas in the city's large market for decades. One woman commented that the sale of tortillas remained constant over time. The biggest change has been the arrival of bus service, making the 10-kilometer trip between the town and the city that much quicker.

San Juan del Estado plots to the right of these three communities and near the point on the graph where the various outcomes intersect. In fact, San Juan del Estado and Guadalupe Etla showed the most diversity in migration outcomes. For these communities, Oaxaca City was a place to find work. Each village was home to a large group of professionals and skilled workers who made the half-hour commute daily to salaried jobs. For example, three households in San Juan del Estado sent members to Oaxaca City, where they had positions as teachers, while nine other individuals held professional positions in businesses based in the city. Men in San Juan del Estado were also employed as taxi drivers and chauffeurs, transporting people between the town and the city. Finally, a large cohort of young people traveled to the city for advanced schooling at the state's university and technological institute. An average of 39% of the households in these four communities sent children to Oaxaca City for higher education (35% of the households in Santa María Guelacé and 30% of the households in Guadalupe Etla also sent students to Oaxaca City).

Guadalupe Etla has excellent transportation services and is a short twenty minutes from Oaxaca City. The town has a growing economic infrastructure of its own, with restaurants, small businesses, an archaeological site (San José el Mogote), and a growing population of Oaxacans who have left the city to live in Guadalupe Etla's more suburban, country setting. In addition, dairy producers in the community did extremely well for themselves and did not necessarily seek out work in Oaxaca City or migration. In fact, no dairy producers sent members to Oaxaca City for work, although half of all dairy producers sent their children to the city for schooling. Dairy producers tended to limit their efforts to dairy production. This was quite different from most rural Oaxacans, who typically combined at least three different work strategies (usually farming with domestic and unskilled wage labor). Finally, less than half of the households that were involved in dairy production had migrant members.

San Martín Tilcajete also plots a little beyond the normal range in the correspondence analysis. The community falls lower on the *y*-axis than most villages, but it is also nearly equidistant between international migrations and nonmigration and near circuit moves on the *x*-axis. San Martín's pattern is explained by the important role of the production of Alebrijes in the local economy. The sale of Alebrijes is an important source of money for San Martín's populace (Chibnik 2003). In fact, as we explored San Martín, we found that a series of variables proved important to the decision to make circuit moves and/or to migrate.

Variables that influenced migration outcomes included the age of the male and female household heads; the presence of artisans; the amount of maize a household produced during a year; a household's weekly expenses; and, not surprisingly, the presence of migrants in familial networks. Circuit movers were typically older men and younger women who were not as likely to be involved in craft production, even though they participated in farming. Migrants, on the other hand, were typically younger men and older women who had relatives and friends already living in the United States or other parts of Mexico. Artisans who were doing well often chose not to migrate. One owner of a small gallery near the center of the town remarked, "Why should I go to the United States? Of course I can earn a lot of money—but how much do I have to spend? It is just too expensive to migrate."

The last community I want to describe is San Juan Guelavia, where we found the highest rate of migration: 62% of all households were involved in some kind of movement. San Juan Guelavia is a Zapotec-speaking community that functioned as a hacienda during much of the late nineteenth and early twentieth centuries (see Mendieta y Núñez 1960). The descendents of the *hacendados* (owners of the hacienda) had continued to live in the community and controlled a good portion of the land. Informants often commented on this history and argued the lack of good arable land (particularly because of the controlling interests of the *hacendado*) had led to the rapid rise in migration rates for the community. The number of Guelavians involved in agricultural labor dropped by more than 38% between 1940 and 1990 (from 621 to 386 individuals). Nevertheless, there was no correlation between land use patterns and migration. Instead, the linkages that Guelavians held with friends and relatives who were migrants were the most important predictors of an individual's move to a U.S. or an internal destination.

Circuit moves in San Juan Guelavia coincided with the kinds of work that individuals pursued. Those community members who sought wage labor in construction went where jobs were available, whether that was

Oaxaca City or a local area. San Juan Guelavia was also home to a small craft industry that produced handmade baskets for sale and export. Unfortunately, the market for the baskets had collapsed, with few sales outside the central valleys. The rising costs of raw materials had forced many producers out of the market. Those who remained complained that they could not earn a wage through production, and for some the alternative appeared to be migration.

What can we learn from the distribution of the various kinds of moves and the communities in the correspondence analysis? First, we note that the moves that households make are not the same. In other words, migration outcomes have specific qualities. Second, although migration occurs in each community, the outcomes of migrations vary among the communities. Third, some communities have similar migration patterns, such as Santa María Guelacé, Guadalupe Etla, San Pedro Ixtlahuaca, and San Juan del Estado, whereas other communities have quite different migration patterns and plot as outliers in the correspondence analysis, such as San Juan del Río, San Juan Guelavia, and Santa Inés Yatzeche.

We cannot reduce these differences, their causes, and where they may lead to single variables. Furthermore, no common historical or ethnographic thread explains the differences. San Juan del Río, San Lorenzo Albarradas, and Santa Inés Yatzeche give the impression that they are more isolated, poorer rural communities. However, even among these communities there are important differences. Santa Inés Yatzeche is an indigenous community, as is San Juan del Río. San Lorenzo Albarradas has lost most of its citizens who speak an indigenous language. Santa Inés Yatzeche is within walking distance of Zimatlán, an important market center for the southern end of the south valley, but does not access that market for wage work. Finally, Villa Díaz Ordaz, though indigenous, is not in as precarious a position as other indigenous communities.

It is probably not possible to develop a model of migration that will concisely explain all of the variation found among households and communities. It is even more difficult to predict future patterns. We cannot select a single independent social, economic, or demographic variable. Nevertheless, I found that it is possible to use a logistical regression to predict future trends (Cohen et al. 2003). However, some basic assumptions needed to be made. First, because the decision to migrate is inherently economic, I chose economic variables from the 259 independent variables available in the data set. Second, because 259 independent variables is far too many to build an effective model, I ran a series of bivariate correlations to deter-

TABLE 3.6 LOGIT REGRESSION PREDICTING THE LIKELIHOOD OF MIGRATION FOR RURAL OAXACANS

	ß	*SE*
members	.083	.057
migfrien	−2.268	.331
goodssc	.097	.036
Intercept	−.775	.655
X^2	100.674	
-2 Log-likelihood	111.882	
Cox & Snell R^2	.269	
Nagelkereke R^2	.359	
N	321	

$p < .05$

		Predicted		
		Are migrants in the household?		
Observed		1	0	*Percentage correct*
Step 1: Are migrants	0	153	29	82.1
in the household?	1	54	105	66.0
Overall percentage				74.1

mine which variables showed an association with migration but would not build multicolinearity.

The result was a list of thirteen independent variables, of which three were significant predictors of migration outcomes:

1. The total of members in the household (*members*)
2. Ties to individuals with migration experience (*migfriend*)
3. The goods and appliances owned by a family (*goodssc*)

The variable *goodssc* tabulated the total number of key consumer goods and appliances present in a household, which included water heater, washing machine, shower, gas/electric stove, refrigerator, television, radio, vehicle, computer, iron, and sewing machine.

The dichotomous variable *migpres*, "Are migrants in the household?" (where 1 = yes and 0 = no), served as the dependent variable in the model. With the three independent variables described above, I achieved a 74% prediction rate (table 3.6). The results suggest that migrants who have friends and relatives with experience as migrants (or settled in the United States) will be more likely to migrate in the future; that larger households are more likely to send migrants; and that households with more resources will more likely send migrants to U.S. destinations in the future.

I am always surprised when I return to Oaxaca and find someone at home who had told me that they would never return. Alternatively, I am just as surprised when a migrant who repeatedly told me he would never leave his home and family again is gone. It is clear that the decision to migrate is profound and is influenced by variables that include the number of children a household must support, the networks the households is linked to, and even the life experiences of the individual in question. However, the decision is not made with perfect knowledge. Instead, the decision to migrate is made by households, with the active participation of household members. The decision takes account of member strengths, the household's resources, and the community's traditions. The decision does not always meet with success. Some migrants disappear, leaving their families to wonder what happened. Other migrants return with little to show for their efforts. Nevertheless, most migrants in the central valleys do succeed and return home to their families and communities. For those who succeed, migration is a critical option. Migration is the way to build a home, to fund a child's education, and to cover the expenses of community participation. Roman Hipolito, who works legally in the United States, mentioned the sweetest possibility to me one afternoon, as we watched a basketball game in Santa Ana:

> Well, for me, you know, all I want is a satellite dish and my beers. I want to come home in a few years and just retire. That would be perfect. I've got my papers, and here I've got my home. So when I'm sixty-five, I'm going to sit here and collect my social security and enjoy my grandkids.
>
> ROMAN HIPOLITO, SANTA ANA DEL VALLE, MAY 1993[4]

Four

MIGRATION, SOCIOECONOMIC CHANGE, AND DEVELOPMENT

Today—well, today, young people are under the illusion that they can get everything if they will just go north. They go north, they work, and then they will have something to buy a nice house, a nice car. But they won't come back, maybe for a fiesta, but they won't come back.

SEÑORA LUISA ESPINOSA, SANTA MARÍA GUELACÉ, JUNE 2000

I spent twenty-eight years in a little adobe house. Then my husband went to Mexico [City], where he worked selling foods with his patron. They worked hard, selling beans, maize, and sugar in their store. He sent money home, he visited, and we had children. He would come home and then leave again. We built this home, but it was not easy. I had my children, my son and daughter. We sent them both to the city [Oaxaca City] to learn, and he kept traveling to Mexico.

SEÑORA FLORA BAUTISTA, SAN JUAN DEL ESTADO, MAY 2001

Our kids were grown and looking for work, and there was just nothing here for them. They needed work and money for their own families. So our sons left, and our daughter left too—she's in Oaxaca [City], working in a small store. Our sons have been in the United States for five or six years. They send back money, but only a little, maybe 1,000 pesos [about US$100] every year. They have their own families to worry about. They bought trucks and fixed their homes.

ANTONIO MARTÍNEZ AND FRANCISCA ÁVILA, SAN JUAN GUELAVIA, JUNE 2001

My two sons have spent many, many years in the United States working. I went there too, first in 1956, when I was only eighteen. I worked as a bracero, and I built this house. Now my sons are there and living with a cousin. Me, I'm here all alone—my poor wife passed away years ago. The boys send money home regularly, and I built them each a home ***[waves to two empty two-story homes just off the main home]****, but look at them—they are so sad and empty.*

VALERIANO GARCÍA, SANTA ANA DEL VALLE, 1996

In chapter 3 we explored what migration and circuit moves looked like in the central valleys, and we noted household patterns and community variation as rural Oaxacans head for destinations in Mexico and in the United States. In this chapter we ask, what motivates the moves. Why are so many rural Oaxacans ready to sacrifice their home life and family in order to migrate? The obvious answer is that most Oaxacan migrants take to the road because they cannot find well-paid wage labor at home. To cover the costs of daily life, people leave their hometowns and head for the border.

Most central valley Oaxacans are more than happy to join in the growing global market, and thus household heads must juggle the demand for goods and services at home against the lack of wage work locally. Migrants are aware that there is little potential for economic growth locally, and they want, or at least perceive that they need, better homes and luxury goods, education for their children, and money to invest in small businesses. Therefore rural Oaxacans leave for Oaxaca City and its booming tourist market, for Mexico City, and for the fields of Sonora and Baja California, or more often they leave for a job in the U.S. service industry. Once they have settled, migrants begin to send money home—they remit to their households. Money flows home mostly by wire and at a high cost to the migrant, but it flows, and millions of dollars are returned to the state's rural communities.[1] Sons and daughters remit to parents; husbands and wives support their children, households, and communities. However, remittance patterns, like migration patterns, are quite varied. Although some migrants remit regularly and follow a neat schedule, others remit infrequently or sometimes not at all. It is also important to remember that receiving households are not consistent in the ways they use remittances.

This chapter focuses on the outcomes of migration and asks, what are the costs and benefits that come from the moves that rural Oaxacans make? I begin with a review of the debate over what remittances mean for rural Oaxaca. Can remittances stimulate development and growth? Or does migration build dependency? Does it rob a community of its able-bodied workers, replacing them with high expectations for local growth that cannot be met? And what can we learn concerning this debate, given remittance patterns in the central valleys? The second part of the chapter considers these issues in terms of what we have learned in Oaxaca.

UNDERSTANDING REMITTANCE PRACTICES

The debate over the positive and negative outcomes of migration and remittance practices is framed by two compelling arguments. On one side are scholars who note the costs of migration and the limited effects of remittance use (see Rempel and Lobdell 1978). This school of thought points out that remittances are used to purchase consumer goods and to cover the costs of daily life and therefore do not contribute to local economic development. On the other side are scholars who argue that the analysis of remittance outcomes is unduly pessimistic and does not take account of household development, the social impacts of remittance behavior, and the strategic ways in which migrant households deploy their remittances to cover daily expenses as well as limited investments (see, for example, Taylor et al. 1996a).

Scholars who argue that migration is a costly decision with few positive outcomes tend to focus on the economic dependency that migration creates. Dependency in this sense means that rural sending communities throughout the developing world become "dependent" upon labor markets, economic cycles, and wages in the developed world for their well-being. In some cases, jobs are exported to the developing world, such as those in the *maquiladoras* (factories) along the U.S.-Mexican border. These factories attract rural migrants from throughout Mexico to their low (but substantially higher than local) wages. Alternatively, in the case of international migration, foreign labor markets attract migrants. In this situation, rural communities become little more than centers where surplus labor can be stored until it is needed (Wilson 2000).

Stuart and Kearney (1981) argued the dependency position. They maintained that U.S.-bound migrants from the Mixteca of Oaxaca (the mountainous region west of the central valleys) created economic dependency in sending communities and, in the process, jeopardized these local communities and local social systems.[2] Brana-Shute and Brana-Shute (1982) developed a similar model for the Caribbean, asserting that most remittances returned by migrants in the United States were spent on consumer goods, real estate, and housing. Furthermore, they stated that the loss of migrants to destination communities was an additional negative impact, one that led to "brain drain" as a region, a community, or even a country watched its able-bodied, young adult workers leave for the promise of higher wages in the United States and western Europe (see Guidi 1993; Rubenstein 1992).

Rural communities and their populations become lost in these increasingly dependent systems. Young adults who want the goods and services they perceive to be the trappings of "modern" life must migrate to find and afford them. In rural Mexico the result is an illness, "migrant syndrome," which addicts rural youth to the "drug" of U.S. cultural and consumer goods.[3] In such a situation, local development cannot take place. Migrants can build homes and water systems and even sponsor fiestas, but if they do not return home, what is the point? A local system cannot survive if it is built around the very young and the very old and the majority of adults are missing.

Sometimes in an interview an informant can say what we anthropologists miss. In this case, Valeriano García, a former *presidente municipal* in Santa Ana, found the words that expressed the pessimism of dependency. In 1993, I spent a few afternoons with him, collecting his life history. He had spent several years working in the United States, first as a bracero in the 1950s and later as an undocumented migrant, working in agriculture and the service industry of Southern California. Over the course of our interviews, I learned that he had used the money he saved to build a beautiful home, to educate his sons, and even to defray some of the costs of holding high office in the village. Nevertheless, he saw migration as a negative force. For him, too many young men and women were leaving the village. Too few returned to the village, and of those that did return, few stayed long enough to participate in the *cargo* system. Over a dinner of beans and rice, he summarized his position in the community for me. "Look at me," he said. "Look at me. I'm an important man in this town. Like all those others. . . . But what am I really? I'm like a big tom turkey; I can dance and show my feathers, but only right here, only right now. I'm nothing beyond right here." It was a sad commentary and one with which I was not entirely comfortable. Nonetheless, Don Valeriano's position resonated with me.

On the other hand, some scholars believe that migration can have positive effects or at least can play a positive role in local social life. Richard Jones (1998) makes the important point that migrant remittances often act as an effective safety net for people who exist outside of the scope and pur-

A tienda *with remittance transfer services, Guadalupe Etla. Author photo.*

view of the state, who lack local wage work, and who are ignored by the international movement of capital and commerce. Jones uses the example of Mexico and argues that migrant remittances are critical to the survival of rural communities. Nevertheless, he cautions that class or classlike differences can divide rural communities along socioeconomic lines and temper the effects of remittances. Dennis Conway and I (1998) made a similar point, suggesting that remittances in Mexico and the Caribbean could have an important positive effect on households, but that success is often tempered by the evolving status of households as they develop over time (see Cohen 2001).

Durand and Massey (1992), working in Zacatecas, Michoacán, and Guanajuato, found that although the bulk of remittances typically go to daily household expenses, home construction, and the purchase of consumer goods, enough remittances go to other kinds of investments that they have a substantial impact on public work projects. Remittances can also contribute to a household's economic security and access to liquid capital (Taylor et al. 1996a, 402).

The impacts of remittances change over time. As migration grows more common and less risky, and as sojourns lengthen and remittances continue, outcomes tend to move from negative to positive (Taylor et al. 1996a, 405). Taylor (1992) tracks these changes in rural Mexico, noting that remittances to rural households between 1982 and 1988 went from having a negative effect on overall income levels (that is, they brought down a household's total income) to having a positive effect (increasing incomes). Specifically, in 1982 every dollar returned by migrants was worth less than US$1 to the migrant's household. By 1988 the value of every dollar returned to a household was nearly doubled and brought US$1.85 of goods and services to that household.

Smith (1998) makes the same point for communities in Puebla and adds that migrant associations can have profound effects on sending communities. Not only do these groups finance local public works projects, but they also support the arts and culture, sending money home to cover the costs of fiestas and school construction. In addition, the political impact of migration and remittances can be profound. Besides returning money to households and communities, migrants also bring back new ideas and can at times capture the attention of the state, as Rivera-Salgado (1999) showed in his work with Mixtec migrant associations in California. Thus the social impacts of migration can be nearly as important as the financial impacts (see Goldring 1998; Kearney 2000; Levitt 1998; Orozco 2002).

A final concern with the outcomes of migration and remittance practices is whether remittances destabilize local social systems and contribute to increasing economic inequality between migrating and nonmigrating households. Massey et al. (1994), in their analysis of continuity and change in nineteen migrant communities, asserted that again we must pay close attention to time as we investigate changes in social and economic inequality. The authors found that status differences between migrant and nonmigrant households are initially quite significant, but that over time they will moderate. Moderation and a decline in inequality should come as the risks and costs of migration decline. Early sojourners are typically from resource-rich households, which can cross the border without undo concern over the costs and risks of movement. As migration becomes a more common occurrence, the costs and risks of movement should decline, and the pool of potential movers should in response increase and grow more diverse. A more diverse migrant pool should ideally lead to a decline in differences among migrant and nonmigrant households, as it becomes relatively easier for nonmigrant households to join the flow of migrants to national and international destinations.

OAXACAN REALITIES

Oaxacan communities lack anything but the most rudimentary of infrastructures. What can remittances accomplish in such a setting? In a household like that of Antonio Martinez and Francisca Avila, where there is no work for growing children, what options are available locally? Does brain drain matter in a place like San Juan Guelavia? And what about local economic development? What does it mean when rural communities cannot turn to the state for support but must ask member households to pool their resources and invest in local infrastructural projects? Given these questions, can we discern patterns in Oaxacan movement that argue for dependency or development? What do migrant remittances actually accomplish? Are younger households more likely to use remittances for daily expenses and home improvements, while older migrant households invest in businesses? Finally, what about the migrant pool itself? Is it growing more diverse?

REMITTANCE PRACTICES IN RURAL OAXACA

Rural Oaxacans in the central valleys are clear about the place and role of migration in their lives and communities. We asked thirty migrant and nonmigrant household heads in Guadalupe Etla, San Martín Tilcajete, and San Juan Guelavia to rank five motivations for migrating to the United States, using a Likert-type scale (Bernard 2002, 308).[4] The five motives for migrating that we asked informants to rank were taken from discussions and interviews we had conducted over three field seasons:

1. To find work
2. To better a family's living conditions
3. To allow a household to save money for a future investment
4. To purchase a specific item
5. To have an adventure

TABLE 4.1 FREQUENCY SCORES FOR MIGRATION MOTIVATIONS

Why do people migrate?	*Frequency score*
To find work	5.2616
To improve the household	5.4019
To save for the future	3.3674
To make a purchase	1.4732
To have an adventure	0.3508

Note: $n = 29$ respondents.

Migrants and nonmigrants ranked "to better a family's living conditions" as an extremely important motive for migration (see table 4.1 for frequency scores for each variable).[5] In fact, 79% of respondents ranked it most important, and 96% ranked it first or second as a motive for migration. A majority of informants (70%) also responded that they would use migration as a way to find work. Only 25% of respondents ranked saving money for future investments as an important motive for migration, and just 27% ranked purchasing a specific item as a reason to migrate. Most interesting was that 60% of respondents believed that an adventure was an inappropriate motive for migration; only 5% (all of whom were individuals with migration experience) believed that an adventure was a good reason to migrate.[6]

The importance of migration for Oaxacans seeking wage-paying positions is clear when we look at the kinds of work that are available locally. We found that 71% of area households rely at least in part on farming to make a living. Nevertheless, only 41% of that total (174 of 420 households) earned enough from farming not to send circuit movers to Oaxaca City or migrants to internal and international destinations. In fact, there is little that Oaxacans can do locally if they want to earn a living wage. Although 60% of paid farmworkers (individuals working on other people's land) stay within their natal villages and do not seek wage work outside the community (earning on average about 50 pesos, US$5, a day), most workers whether unskilled or skilled must seek positions in Oaxaca City or beyond. Only 11% of professionals, 28% of teachers, 25% of skilled workers, and 32% of businesspeople, paid domestics, and unskilled laborers (construction workers) find wage work within their home communities. Thus circuit moves and migration are critical for obtaining work.

A second question, also using a five-point Likert-type scale, asked informants to rank the ways in which they might use migrant remittances. We gave informants the following options:

1. To cover daily costs of living
2. To cover shortfalls from local wage work
3. To construct or improve a home
4. To cover educational expenses for children
5. To participate in local fiestas
6. To make specific purchases
7. To purchase land
8. To purchase stock animals
9. To save for future use or investments
10. To pay for medical expenses

Here the responses clustered around specific outcomes (see table 4.2 for frequencies). The majority of informants ranked covering the costs of living as the first (81%) or second (9%) most important reason to migrate and remit; building or improving a home was also ranked as the first (30%) or second (40%) most important reason to migrate and remit. Informants considered migration and the resulting remittances to be an important source of cash for a household, and many of them ranked using migration as a means to cover shortfalls in income first (36 percent) or second (45 percent). Mi-

TABLE 4.2 FREQUENCY SCORES FOR THE POTENTIAL USE OF REMITTANCES

If I received remittances, I would buy/pay for . . .	*Frequency score*
Costs of living	5.753
Work security	2.385
Home construction/renovation	4.630
Education	2.315
Fiestas	−2.245
Large purchases	1.473
Land purchases	1.613
Stock animal purchases	0.631
Savings	1.543
Medical care	2.526

Note: $n = 29$ respondents.

A traditional kitchen, Santa María Guelacé. Author photo.

grating to secure the money necessary to cover fiesta expenses ranked low for all informants, and no one ranked it as a first or second priority. Instead, 13 percent of informants were neutral about using migration as a means to cover fiesta expenses, and the rest maintained that it was an inappropriate practice.

Saving remittances for investment in a business ranked somewhat higher but received only mild support, with 50% of informants ranking it as an appropriate secondary use of a migrant's remittances. Thirty-six percent of informants ranked migrating to earn money for a specific purchase as second or third in importance, and 20% thought that migrating to earn money for medical expenses was also somewhat important.

When we asked informants to rank specific remittance outcomes, the results were largely consistent with our questions concerning motivations for migration. We asked informants to rank ten possible outcomes or uses for their remittances again using a five-point, Likert-type scale. The outcomes informants ranked included the following:

1. To cover daily costs of living
2. To construct or improve a home
3. To cover educational expenses for children

4. To make specific purchases
5. To save for future use or investments
6. To pay for medical expenses

Here, too, responses consistently focused on consumption and construction as viable and important uses of remittances (see table 4.3), with 92% of respondents ranking "to cover daily costs" as the most important use of remittances. Purchasing land and investing in business earned the most diverse responses, and using remittances to cover ritual expenses received the most negative response (65% chose it as an inappropriate use of remittances).

The responses of informants to these general questions concerning their motivations for migration and their plans for their remittances paralleled the actual uses of remittances we collected in our survey for the central valleys rather well. In our surveys, we first asked informants if migrants returned remittances. We then asked informants to describe the schedules that migrants followed for returning remittances and to describe how their remittances were used. Finally, we asked informants to tell us how much money they received in remittances and how remittances were transferred to households from other parts of Mexico and the United States.

Households used remittances in much the way they talked about them in the abstract, with most remittances going to the cover the costs of daily life and the construction or improvement of households (see table 4.4 for actual uses). However, there were some differences. First, in the abstract, no

TABLE 4.3 FREQUENCY SCORES FOR THE SPECIFIC USES OF REMITTANCES

Specific outcomes of remittances	*Frequency score*
Food	6.735
Building materials	5.753
Education	5.682
Purchases	4.209
Business investments	4.770
Medical services	5.051

Note: $n = 29$ respondents.

TABLE 4.4 HOW REMITTANCES WERE INVESTED

Remittance use	*No. of responses*[a]
No remittances received	60 (14%)
Daily expenses	187 (44%)
Home construction/renovation	71 (17%)
Education	27 (6%)
Purchase of domestic items	16 (4%)
Ritual expenses	8 (2%)
Health care	6 (1%)
Purchase of agricultural/farm goods	2 —
Business startup and expansion	22 (5%)
Land purchase	7 (2%)
Other	17 (4%)

[a] Total is less than 100% because of rounding

one commented that a household might not receive remittances. In practice, we found that just over 13% of migrant households that commented on their remittances practices acknowledged that some migrating members did not remit. Nonremitters included new migrants who had not yet found work or had yet to cover the expenses of their trips. Second, in the abstract, health care and education figured as more important uses of remittances than either did in reality. Finally, no one said they were saving remittances for future emergencies.

The household heads we interviewed spoke hopefully of the future and of the money they anticipated that their children and spouses would soon return. Nonremitters were usually migrants who had established families in the United States or other parts of Mexico and were preoccupied with their own finances to the exclusion of their natal households. Typically, informants would explain the loss in terms similar to these:

> Our sons left years ago, and for a while they sent money home. But over time the money slowed down. Now we get something here, something there, but the boys have their own families and their own problems. They don't send money any longer.
>
> DOÑA ANTONIA MATADAMAS, SAN JUAN DEL ESTADO, MAY 2000

This finding was not a surprise and follows what Lowell and de la Garza (2002, 20) assert is a typical pattern of decline.

Households that acknowledged receiving remittances used them for two specific practices. First was the daily support of the household, and second was home construction or renovation. In total, 44% of migrant households reported using at least some of their remittances to cover daily expenses (food, transportation, clothing, and so forth), while 17% also used remittances to cover the costs of home construction and renovation. A small group, just over 5% of central valley households, used some of their remittances for business startups, just over 1% invested their remittances in land, and less than 1% used remittances for farm-related purchases.

Covering the costs of food, clothing, transportation, and incidentals was included with every other remittance use category, except for the purchase of agricultural/farm goods. We found that 77% of the migrant households that earmarked their remittances for business startup and expansion still used some of those remittances for daily expenses, and 71% of migrant households that used remittances to cover land purchases also used remittances to cover daily expenses. Additionally, 100% of the households that used some of their remittances for health care also used some of their funds to cover daily household expenses. The point here is that rural households depend upon remittances for their daily success, and only a very few households can earmark more than a small portion of their remittances for use in areas other than daily expenses, purchases, and business startups.

REMITTANCE PRACTICES AND COMMUNITY DIFFERENCES

The ways in which central valley households use their remittances argue for what dependency advocates would characterize as noninvestment outcomes. Remittances go to cover the costs of living, the purchase of consumer goods, and the improvement of living standards rather than to support economically viable businesses and/or the creation of local wage labor alternatives. However, a more complex set of outcomes and possibilities is apparent if we break down remittance use patterns by community (table 4.5).

First, covering daily expenses was important in each community and accounted for much if not the majority of all remittances, no matter the location. However, with the exception of San Pablo Huitzo, Santa Inés Yatzeche, Santa María Guelacé, and San Pedro Ixtlahuaca, at least 10% of

TABLE 4.5 REMITTANCE USE BY COMMUNITY (%)

Community	*No remittances*	*Daily expense*	*Home construction/ renovation*	*Education*	*Purchase of consumer goods*	*Business investment*	*Land investment*	*Purchase of farm goods*	*Ritual expenses*	*Health care*	*Other*
Villa Díaz Ordaz	10	54	12	2	2	10	2			2	2
Guadalupe Etla	3	40	33	10	3	3			7		
Santa Inés Yatzeche	35	40	5	5	5				10		
San Juan del Estado	10	41	16	8	2	2	2	2	6	2	8
San Juan Guelavia	8	43	22	8	6	3	2			2	6
San Juan del Río	21	39	21	4		14					
San Lorenzo Albarradas	14	67	10				5	5			
Santa María Guelacé	8	69	8	8							5
San Martín Tilcajete	31	31	19	10	1	1	1		1	3	1
San Pablo Huitzo		80		10	10						
San Pedro Ixtlahuaca	9	40	9	2	12	16					12

remittances went to home construction and renovation expenses. House building and renovation are not true investments, for they do not contribute to market expansion or foster profits in the household. Nevertheless, many families used their new and renovated homes (or at least rooms in these homes) as workshops/galleries or *tiendas* (small dry-goods stores).[7] This was particularly true in Guadalupe Etla, where the local economy was growing partly because urban Oaxacans were relocating to the village. Home building and renovations also fostered the growth and expansion of local contractors—the small firms that did the building and planned the renovations (Adelman et al. 1988; Massey et al. 1998). In most villages, we found that at least one if not more households had opened small firms to meet the demand for home building and renovation services.

A second pattern that was clear in the community-based data was the large percentage of migrant households that did not receive remittances in Santa Inés Yatzeche, San Martín Tilcajete, and San Juan del Río. In Santa Inés Yatzeche, 35% of the migrants who had left the community did not remit regularly; in San Martín Tilcajete, 31% of the migrants did not remit; and in San Juan del Río, 21% of the migrants did not remit.

The history of movement may explain the relatively higher percentages of nonremitters in these communities. First, as the migration process matures and as migrants age, remittance rates tend to fall. Lowell and de la Garza (2002, 19) note that remittances decline by an average of 2% for every 1% of additional time migrants stay in their destination communities. At the same time, migrants who are among the first to leave a community and are in the early phases of their sojourns face more risks and costs as they cross the border (Massey 1990).

Migration in San Martín Tilcajete has a long history. It dates to the 1930s and has continued through each decade since, with a steady flow of new migrants throughout the late 1970s, the 1980s, and the 1990s. Thus migration has had plenty of time to mature in the village. Alternatively, Santa Inés Yatzeche and San Juan del Río have much shorter histories of migration. The first migrants left Santa Inés Yatzeche in 1988, with the bulk leaving only after 1998. In San Juan del Río the first migrant left in 1985, with the majority of migrants leaving only after 1994. Sojourns were also quite a bit longer for migrants who originated in San Martín Tilcajete, averaging just under 9 years, whereas migrants from Santa Inés Yatzeche averaged only about 3.5 years away and San Juan del Río's migrants, just under 5.5 years.

These trends suggest three reasons why San Martín Tilcajete's migrants were less likely to remit. First, migrants had been away from their community long enough for the ties to their households to have weakened substantially, thus reducing the pressure for remittances; and second, the history of migration in the community was long enough that virtually all households were linked to migrants, so the overall utility of migration had declined. Furthermore, nearly anyone from the community could travel to the United States if necessary, rather than depending on remittances (Massey et al. 1994).

Migration in Santa Inés Yatzeche and San Juan del Río was still relatively new and included a much smaller population. Migration had not yet reached a point of equilibrium, and the costs of migration remained high. Thus remittances were limited by the combined effects of the relatively smaller total number of years that any one migrant spent away from the natal household and the limited history that migration had in the community in general.

Cultural concerns also affect migration and the lack of remitting in San Martín Tilcajete. Because migration is relatively less costly in San Martín Tilcajete, nearly anyone who wants to leave the village can elect to do so. Individuals who want to "exit" their household and give up their membership face few limitations if they do so (see Hirschman 1970). Several of the household heads we interviewed complained about abandonment by children and described migration in largely negative terms. Additionally, the success of San Martín Tilcajete's artisans meant that migrants were under less pressure to remit and could migrate for reasons other than the support of their families. In fact, some households noted that people from the community migrated not to find work but instead to find markets for locally made crafts and to sell those crafts directly to consumers.

A third pattern is reflected by the diversity of remittance use patterns that we found in several communities. San Juan del Estado and San Martín Tilcajete had the most diverse patterns of remittance use, followed closely by San Juan Guelavia and Villa Díaz Ordaz, whereas San Pablo Huitzo was the least diverse in remittance patterns. The diversity of outcomes likely relates to the history and size of the migrant pools in these communities. These communities had large migrant pools, histories that included migrants leaving in the first half of the twentieth century, and migrants who had been away for more years than average (although the length of stay is short in Guadalupe Etla). San Martín Tilcajete was home to the first migrant in the sample who left the central valleys in 1930. San Juan Guelavia's first migrant left for the United States in 1941. Migrants from San Juan del Estado joined this slow but steady flow of migrants in 1956. San Martín Tilcajete's very healthy craft economy also allowed migrant households to be more creative with their remittances.

Business investments were highest in San Pedro Ixtlahuaca, San Juan del Río, and Villa Díaz Ordaz, but the total percentage of remittances given over to business was small (about 8% of the funds returned). Business investments reflected different opportunities in each village. Households in San Juan del Río used some of their remittances to enter the mescal market, while families in Villa Díaz Ordaz invested in craft production. In San Pedro Ixtlahuaca, businesses were growing to serve urban Oaxacans who entered the village as they built new homes.

REMITTANCE INCOMES AND HOUSEHOLD EXPENSES

In general, we have noted that the remittance practices in the central valleys, whether we focus on households or communities, tend to be concentrated on uses associated with daily life and consumption, with a much smaller percentage of remittances going directly to business investments. A question that comes to mind, given these patterns, is, just how much money are we talking about? In general, remittances were not large for the area.

Migrants traveling to national destinations remitted on average just over 700 pesos (US$70) a month over a seven-year period. However, one-half of all national migrants remitted no more than 100 pesos (US$10) a month over a three-year period. There was also a difference between the remittances returned by migrant men and women. Although migrant men returned an average of 650 pesos (about US$65) a month, women returned just 500 pesos (US$50).

Remittances from migrants traveling to U.S. destinations averaged just over US$300 a month over a six-year period, but again one-half of those migrants returned no more than US$200 a month for only about one year.[8] Migrant women who moved to the United States also typically remitted less than migrant men did. The women remitted US$130 a month on average, while migrant men averaged US$280 per month. This difference reflected the lower wages that women are paid for their work, even though about half of all the men and women surveyed found jobs in the service industries; and it also reflected the fact that 12% of the men surveyed had found relatively higher wages (up to US$20 per hour) working in construction. Finally, migrant women were expected to care for their migrant households, and this added domestic work took time away from the jobs they could hold.

Most migrants who are in the United States have several potential means through which they can remit. In the past, before the advent of electronic wire service, many migrants hoarded their savings and carried them home in their pockets. The dangers of such a system are obvious and include theft as well as loss. Nevertheless, older migrants who began their migrations in the 1950s and 1960s often continued to carry their savings home. Younger migrants typically chose to wire money home, and the majority of migrants used Western Union. Most market towns in the central valleys and some of the communities we surveyed had Western Union offices or a bank that could handle a wire transfer. But such transfers are extremely costly for the migrant, with fees ranging as high as 20% of the total transfer (see Martin 1996). A few migrants said they would give money to a friend and ask him or her to deliver it home. We did not encounter any migrants who said they had been victims of theft on either side of the border, but it was a constant point of concern and tension for migrants and their families.[9]

Migrants who stayed in their destination communities for more than a few years earned a good deal more than the average migrant did (although the mean is about US$500 a month, 75% of all migrants return less than US$400). Migrants who remitted more than US$500 a month tended to stay in the United States for more than five years. Internal migration patterns were similar. Internal migrants who remitted more than 1,000 pesos a month were involved in moves that took them away from the central valleys for no less than six years, and some continued to work as migrants for up to thirty years.

What do these remittances mean for area households? We asked informants to estimate their weekly incomes (not including remittances), as well as their weekly expenses. We were able to check at least some of these estimates against responses we received concerning wages and incomes from work. Expenses for area households were harder to estimate, but we were able to ask community leaders what services and commodities cost in each village.

Weekly incomes for area households ranged from a low of nothing (6% of households) to highs of 3,000 to 7,000 pesos a week. High-income households (3% of area households) included professionals from San Juan del Estado and Guadalupe Etla, a butcher living in Guadalupe Etla who had spent time as a migrant, and artisans in San Martín Tilcajete. Still, weekly incomes averaged just over 700 pesos, with half of all households making no more than 600 pesos. There were little average income differences between migrant and nonmigrant households. Incomes for migrant households averaged 769 pesos a week, while nonmigrant households averaged 715 pesos a week.

Weekly expenses ranged from nothing to 6,000 pesos a week. A family with no income laughed when I asked them about their weekly expenses. "What do we spend in a week? Whatever God will give us!" said Marco Martínez in San Juan del Estado. "I make what I can, but too many weeks I don't earn a thing. Weeks like that I'll trade my time for food or cover someone's *tequio* to earn a little." Households like the Martínezes are the exceptions; only about 5% of area households stated that they had no expenses for the week during which we surveyed them. Just under 2% of households reported that they spent more than 2,000 pesos a week on food, transportation, utilities, schooling, and so forth. The average for area households was just over 400 pesos a week, with half of all households spending no more than 300 pesos a week. Expenses for migrant and nonmigrant households were quite different. Nonmigrant households spent on average 405 pesos a week on their expenses, whereas migrant households spent an average of 553 pesos a week. Combining this information with data from incomes showed that migrant households tended to earn a little more per week than nonmigrating households did (not including remittances), but migrating households also tended to have somewhat higher expenses. The addition of remittances, even if we use a low estimate such as US$200 a month over a year, greatly enhances the economic strength of a migrant household.

REMITTANCES AND INVESTMENT

So far we have noted that the majority of remittances go toward daily expenses and home construction, but what about the small group of households (about 8% of the total) that invest their remittances, start or expand businesses, or purchase land and farm implements for commercial agriculture? Martín Gutiérrez, a fifty-year-old widower and father of five from San Juan Guelavia, described what can happen when a migrant is able to use some of his earnings for business. "When I was young, I went to the United States to build my house. I worked as a carpenter for a lot of years, and I saved about 4,000 pesos, which I used to build this house." As Martín's sons grew older, they replaced their father as migrants.

> My two younger sons left last year, and they send 100 dollars each monthly. The other has stopped sending money. The

> balance of migration is negative, because the migrants are in danger and they learn terrible things. It is better if kids stay at home in their villages and work. I have to work hard to take care of our family and organize our expenses. When my older son helped, it was easier. I saved much of his money for building his home. My daughter used some of that money to start her beauty salon. We bought a little pump to get water too. To save money, we are buying used clothes. . . . My neighbors helped my sons get to the United States. They gave them gifts to cover their expenses, and they fed them while they traveled.
>
> MARTÍN GUTIÉRREZ, SAN JUAN GUELAVIA, DECEMBER 2001

Señor Gutiérrez's story is not surprising. Migrants often leave their home with serious goals in mind, and most migrants, even if they do not use their remittances for investment, are at least thinking about the possibility. Furthermore, migrants use some of their remittances as investment capital once they have covered immediate expenses, constructed or renovated a home, and sent children to Oaxaca City for their continued education.

Migrant households that planned to invest some of their remittances sent on average two members—and as many as four members—to the United States. Migrants from these households stayed in the United States much longer than the typical Oaxacan migrant from the central valleys, and their sojourns averaged 12.5 years. Most of these migrants made two trips to the United States rather than the more typical single sojourn, and 31% (7 of 22) made three to six trips to the United States. Finally, investment-minded migrants remitted at rates much higher than did the average international mover. The seventeen households that described themselves as planning for business startups and expansions averaged remittances of about US$200 per month over the course of their entire migrations.

The expenses and exigencies of everyday life make it hard to hoard remittances and save them for future investments.[10] Internal migrants who remitted more than US$400 a month were involved in moves that took them away from the central valleys for no less than six years, and some continued to work as migrants for as many as thirty years. Some households consciously decide to use their remittances to purchase goods that they could not consume, such as construction materials, goods to fill a small store, or a *yunta* that could be rented for farmwork and hauling.

Households that planned to use their remittances to start or expand a business tended to be smaller (with five or fewer members) and to own substantial amounts of land (nearly 3 hectares on average). The houses of these families also tended to be smaller but built of brick or cement instead of adobe, with finished concrete floors, tile roofs, and kitchens that include gas stoves and sometimes running water.

Business opportunities in central valley communities are quite limited, and as noted above, most of these communities lack the infrastructures to support economic investment and expansion. The marginal costs to start a business, particularly something that demands access to utilities and water, are quite high. Thus households that want to use remittances to invest in businesses tend to establish small stores, beauty salons, repair shops, taxi and trucking services, restaurants, and, in Guadalupe Etla and San Pedro Ixtlahuaca, Internet cafés.[11] Other households invest in agriculture or land and farm implements. One household in Santa María Guelacé used remittances to purchase a *yunta.* "I can earn 500 pesos a day renting out my *yunta* during planting and again during the harvest," Arturo Sáenz told me during an interview in 2000. Three households (two in San Juan del Estado and one in San Pedro Ixtlahuaca) used a portion of their remittances to hire agricultural workers. Don Arturo Martínez of San Pedro Ixtlahuaca reasoned, "Well, I pay these guys 50 pesos a day [500 pesos a week for two workers] for a few weeks here and there, but my son sends us about US$500 every other month." The result will not make Don Arturo's household wealthy, but Don Arturo does not work as hard and he can use his son's remittances to put the household ahead.

REMITTANCES AND COMMUNITY DEVELOPMENT

The increase in wage labor and remittances and in the amount of cash present in area households has led to an increasing reliance on *cooperación* in central valley communities, according to local informants.[12] The importance of *cooperación* and community-supported development cannot be overestimated. The arrival of electricity in the 1970s and paved roads in the 1970s and 1980s, as well as the expansion of water systems and sewers at present, were brought about largely through the efforts and resources of rural populations. The state sometimes supports rural development through programs like Solidaridad;[13] however, the bulk of the money needed to finance most projects continues to come from rural households.

Development is not easy to organize in rural Oaxaca. Often what seems like a sensible goal to one set of households appears as little more than folly to another. One older man from Santa Ana talked to me about the arrival of electricity in their community in the 1970s:

> It was extremely hard to bring electricity to the town. The leaders and the elderly members of that time resisted electrification for many years. I can still recall the voice of my jefe: 'Why do I need more than a candle?' and 'what will a light accomplish but make us waste even more of our money?' It was a difficult period and one when we struggled for a long time.
>
> ELIODORO GARCÍA, SANTA ANA DEL VALLE, JANUARY 1993

Citizens throughout the central valleys continue to debate whether public services should be extended, whether water systems should be expanded, and how best to install sewer systems. Each of these changes costs money, and usually funds are collected locally and requested from households in the form of *cooperación.* The money for projects promoted by community leaders is hard to find locally. One elderly man said, "Oh my, we used to cooperate with a peso or 2 or 10, but now it is 100 pesos here, 50 pesos there. It really adds up!" The importance of *cooperación* is evident in its many uses. *Cooperación* is collected for projects that range from the simple to the complex, from supporting after-school programs for youth to digging a sewer system. Community events, such as village-wide fiestas, are also funded in part through *cooperación.* Most household heads recalled participating in three or four episodes of *cooperación* a year; however, some wealthy households would contribute more often, while poorer households lacking incomes would often negotiate to make their donations in kind rather than in cash. Of the households we talked with concerning *cooperación* ($n = 349$), we found that 76% participated by contributing an average of 400 pesos for the last collection organized in their community. There was little difference in the rates of contribution between nonmigrant and migrant households; 76% of 165 nonmigrant households and 75% of 184 migrant households participated. Nonmigrant households averaged higher payments over time than their migrant counterparts did; however, the difference was not significant.

Cooperación is not a motivation for migration; rather *cooperación* is one way that households use remittances. In fact, although a few migrants mentioned that the savings from their migrations made it easier for them to participate in community government (*cargos* and *comites*), in interviews no one said that service alone was a sufficient motivation for migration. Migrants asserted that an added benefit of remittances was to be able to support community expenses occasionally. The exception to this rule were several older men in Santa Ana del Valle, San Martín Tilcajete, and San Juan Guelavia who were serving in *cargos* and used remittances from their children specifically to cover the expenses of their offices.

A second concern is whether migration may reduce participation in community government, even as *cooperación* supports local development. Several informants voiced this concern and stated that migration was chipping away at local *cargo* systems and reducing levels of *servicio* among citizens. The *presidentes municipales* of San Juan del Estado maintained that migration made it hard for them to find volunteers to fill positions in the local civil hierarchies. We also heard similar complaints from citizens concerning migration during interviews. In an interview in 2001, Guadalupe Sáenz of Santa Inés Yatzeche commented, "We used to be very united. We used to work together. Now we don't work so hard or together. No one comes for *tequio*. Everyone is busy, and everyone has a business. The authority won't call *tequio*."

Despite such stories, we found no relationship between migration and a decline in service participation throughout the valleys. We collected service records for 219 households. Migrant and nonmigrant households were evenly divided, with 42% of nonmigrant and 45% of migrant households participating in their systems. And for the 174 households for which we were able to collect detailed records of service, there was again little difference between migrant and nonmigrants.

DISCUSSION AND CONCLUSION

I began this chapter by asking why Oaxacans from the central valleys are ready to sacrifice their home lives for an opportunity to migrate. I suggested that the easy answer was that they are looking for work and hoping to improve the status of their households. The data presented in this chapter make this position quite clear. Rural Oaxacans talk about their migration decisions as built around two key concerns: the need for wage work and the hope of a better life at home. Their actions emphasize just how important these two factors are when it comes to migration decision making. No outcome colors the choice of migration more than their perception that a better life can be found through migration. Thus husbands and wives travel to national and international destinations in an effort to earn incomes that are not available locally. Migrants to the United States are able to secure jobs that pay well more than the wages they might find locally or in Oaxaca City. They send home whatever they can, minus the fees and service charges.

Remittances tend to go to cover a household's immediate daily expenses. This is certainly the case for the households we encountered. In general, rural Oaxacans from the central valleys are making short-term, almost commuter-like migrations. Typically, they stay in the United States for a year, perhaps two, and then return home. Furthermore, the majority do not remain in the United States long enough to amass or remit the kind of money that would have a long-term effect at home. Rather, remittances supplement what are generally lower weekly incomes, and they make it possible for the nonmigrating members of the household to survive and perhaps even enhance their situations. Remittances also support home construction and renovations, but again the returns are short-term and typically do not extend beyond the construction project.

We found a small group of migrants whose remittances go to investments. These migrants spend more time as migrants but are able therefore to remit more and for longer periods. Nonmigrating members of these households have time to adjust their activities and redistribute their energies to cover for migrating members. The pressure to adapt is less intense for the nonmigrant members when migrants leave for short-term sojourns. They know that the migrants will not be gone for long (usually no more than a year), and rather than learning a new repertoire of coping skills, they can hold on until their migrating member returns.

Given the patterns that we found among migrants in terms of their remittance practices, what can we say about dependency and development? The outcomes of migration in the central valleys appear to share more with a dependency model than with the more positive development model. Wage positions are not available locally, and the majority of workers, whether skilled or unskilled, must leave their hometowns for work. The outcome for the central valleys is that locals leave to escape their communities and what they perceive to be a lack of employment opportunities at home. Migrants do not want to leave—at least that is what we heard in our interviews—yet they have few choices. Where can a professional find work in a community with no industrial base? He or she must go to Oaxaca City or migrate—there are few alternatives.

Remittances also follow what might best be thought of as a "dependency trajectory," with the bulk going to support daily expenses, construction, and the purchase of consumer goods rather than investments in business, land, or the like. However, the remittance patterns also show some positive signs. Rural Oaxacans use their remittances to support the improvement of their communities, and they invest in the development of water delivery systems and sewer service, among other infrastructural improvements. Better homes with finished floors and modern kitchens also have important health outcomes for the rural populace; although we do not have concise evidence in terms of health status, informants describe the situation as improving rapidly throughout the central valleys. Finally, communities continue to rely on traditional systems of organization to manage civil life in their communities. *Cargos, tequio,* and *cooperación* remain quite viable in each village we visited. We noted that, in general, migrant households are as equally involved as nonmigrant households in these systems.

We can also ask about the migrant pool. Is it more diverse than in the past, and are the costs of migration declining, thus allowing more migrants to leave? Although migration has increased rapidly in the region, it remains an expensive proposition, particularly for households whose members are not well connected to migrants who either already live in destination communities or can at the very least supply contacts there. Thus the pool of migrants is more diverse than it was twenty years ago. However, from a national perspective, it is not as diverse as we might expect, and many households cannot afford the costs and risks of migration. The exceptions are communities like San Juan Guelavia, where migration has a longer history and where migration and remittance practices are more diverse.

Finding the key to understanding whether dependency or development will rule the day in the central valleys is likely only possible through the continued analysis of migration and remittance practices over time. Migration has come to dominate social affairs only in the last few decades. It may be a few more decades before we can be sure of the trajectory of these outcomes. The extremes are obvious. Rita López, a widow in San Lorenzo Albarradas, emphasized the negatives that haunt migration for most rural Oaxacans: "Being a migrant is not in general a good idea. It is very risky, and migrants learn bad habits, like taking drugs and joining gangs. They forget their homes and families." On the other hand, there are many if not more households whose members have had good migration experiences and see the evidence daily as they enjoy their renovated, two-story homes with running water and satellite television.

Five NONMIGRANT HOUSEHOLDS

I don't have much experience with migration to the United States. I would like to go and earn some money to support my family, but I cannot. . . . How can I afford it? I have nothing! [Shrugs and laughs.]

JULIO MÉNDEZ CRUZ, GUADALUPE ETLA, JANUARY 2002

You know, I am happy here. I have my store [a **papelería**—*stationery and paper goods store—with the only copying machine in the village], and I think we do well. My brother, he went to the other side and came back. He helps my parents, but I have done this [built the store] myself. I am not interested in migrating; I do not want a husband or children. I just want to do my job. I serve the village, and I am proud of what I have done.*

CLAUDIA LÓPEZ, SAN JUAN GUELAVIA, JANUARY 2002

Migration is really contradictory, a great contradiction. If you manage to earn some money, you won't come home. Or you'll start to drink or waste your money. So what is the point? I don't want to leave my family without support. I don't want to travel so far, and if I did, and if I earned some money—well, then, I would have to pay back the **coyote** *[smuggler] for maybe six months or a year, and I won't save any money. If I do save some money, I'll just spend it in a month or two, so then I have to go back. It is not for me.*

RAMÓN VILLA, SAN JUAN GUELAVIA, JANUARY 2002

A focus on migration patterns and remittance uses in the central valleys can make it appear that these communities are rapidly depopulating as people leave for national and international destinations. Newspaper, radio, and television reports, talk on the street, even the casual comment at a professional meeting, typically focus on migration and suggest that Mexico is becoming a country whose rural communities act as nurseries on the one hand or senior centers on the other. Although there are communities throughout the country where this is the case, many rural Mexicans choose to remain in their hometowns.

Given the pull of jobs in the United States, the lack of wage labor at home, and the desire to better a household's material and social status, why did about 40 percent of the central valley households we visited choose not to migrate?[1] This chapter looks at why Oaxacans remain in their hometowns. Three elements frame and influence the decision to migrate: the social networks available to the household, the socioeconomic status of the household, and the natural resources of the community.

Most studies of migration note that kin ties and social networks are critical to successful movement, and that is certainly the case in Oaxaca. In fact, as will become clear in the next section, social contacts based in kinship and friendship are central to the decisions of most migrants and the lack of such networks limits nonmigrants.

A second important element is the socioeconomic status of the household. It is hardly surprising that poorer households, lacking incomes and without resources (whether social or economic), do not migrate. More surprising are those households that are relatively comfortable by local standards and yet choose not to migrate. There is also a group of households that have relatively high incomes and control enough resources to make migration unnecessary.

Julio Méndez Cruz's household is a good example of the first group. His household lacks connections to migrants and is too poor to afford the risks and costs of migration. Poor households cannot organize the resources necessary to cross the border, and they may even lack the resources to cover internal movements. The problem is not just that they lack the money to cover the costs of movement; they also lack the social networks that are crucial to successful migration. Crossing the border and finding a job are daunting tasks even for the migrant with the resources necessary to support his or her movement. To a household that lacks economic resources as well as social capital, crossing the border can seem nearly impossible.[2]

The household of Claudia López and Ramón Villa is an example of the second group—they hold the resources necessary to migrate, yet they elect to remain at home. Households like these are able to choose their path. Migration, whether to an internal destination or to the United States, is a pos-

Women selling vegetables in Santa Inés Yatzeche, 2002. Author photo.

sibility, but it is not inevitable. These households control enough resources to cover daily expenses and earn enough to be comfortable. These are not wealthy households and they may not be extremely successful; nevertheless, they do not need the supplemental income that migration might offer. These nonmigrants live well, according to their own standards. Migration may be an option in the future, but for the moment, they do not concern themselves with the risks that come with national or international moves.

A smaller set of households is able to move beyond being comfortable and to become quite successful without migrating. Typically, these wealthy nonmigrant households have parlayed landholdings, dairy production, and local business accomplishment into the kind of success that makes migration unnecessary.

The Delgado-Morales household from Santa María Guelacé is a good example of this third group. The household includes five members, all of whom contribute labor and pool resources. The male household head and two sons are involved in agriculture, farming 5 hectares of irrigated land. They produce vegetables for sale, and grow about half of the maize they need for the year. The female household head, Doña Antonia, and her daughter are involved in domestic work around the home. Three times a week, Doña Antonia travels to local markets to sell produce. The key to the household's wealth is the sale of animals, including *yuntas.* Don Gregorio, the male head, is known for training *yuntas,* and his teams bring a high price. By pooling their efforts and carefully managing their resources, the household not only survives but also has grown wealthy without turning to migration.

Geography and natural resources are also critical to migrants and nonmigrants. As was noted in chapter 3, distance is a critical factor to circuit movers; communities that are closer to Oaxaca City can access the city and its labor market far more easily than distant communities. Thus one would expect that nonmigrants in a place like San Pedro Ixtlahuaca make their decision to "stay home" because they can travel to the city to find work. People in a community like Santa Inés Yatzeche or San Juan del Río are in a different situation. Because the trip to Oaxaca City is long and expensive, migrating may be a better decision, and in fact, this has happened.

A focus on nonmigrants helps us gain a sense of the role of migration in the central valleys. It also helps us determine just what migration is at a theoretical level. In this sense, understanding why households do not migrate is as important as understanding why other households do migrate. First, nonmigrant households share kin and communal networks, cultural traditions, social practices, and community resources with most migrant households, and these resources are fundamental to any household's success (Conway 2000, 207). Second, examining the management of assets in nonmigrant households offers a material and socioeconomic foundation upon which we can understand the linkages (or articulations) that characterize transnational space for migrant households (Basch et al. 1994, 81; Kearney 1996).

When I started my investigation of migration in Santa Ana del Valle in 1996, I assumed that I would find a high rate of out-migration and the development of strong transnational networks. These networks would link migrants from Santa Ana to destinations in the United States and would be much like the patterns discovered by Runsten and Kearney (1994) in their study of Mixtec farmworkers (see also Rivera-Salgado 1999). However, I did not find a strong sense of "transnationalism" among Santañeros with whom I worked. Rather, I found that Santañeros were moving between their home village and the United States for economic reasons, and the links between village and individual migrant were built largely around kin ties.

To better understand what migration and transnationalism mean in the central valleys, I added data from eleven other communities (the data presented in this book). The results emphasized the rapid increase in migration from the central valleys in general, as Oaxacans sought regular and higher wages for their work. I also found that kin networks were a cornerstone of much migrant achievement. In other words, the social networks that tied

TABLE 5.1 FREQUENCY SCORES FOR PERCEIVED IMPEDIMENTS TO MIGRATION

Perceived impediment	*Frequency score*
Family	4.7705
Work	3.0868
Village	2.5957
Age of the migrant	3.5779
Health of the migrant	3.0868
Migrant is a woman	2.1748
Parents' concerns	2.0345
Costs of migration	2.9465
Dangers of crossing border	3.9988

Note: $n = 29$ respondents.

migrants together and to their sending households were vital to success in the United States. Critical to understanding these networks is the fact that they are based in ties of kinship, not community. Thus we can perhaps argue that, at the household level, rural Oaxacans from the central valleys are transnational. Whether their communities fall into that category as well is still to be discovered.

The importance of social networks is clear if we examine their place in the decision to migrate. When we asked twenty-nine household heads to use a Likert-type scale to rank items that might hinder migration, we found that family was critical (table 5.1).

We found that 58% of rural Oaxacans believed that a family's status (the strength of its social networks and resources) was a very important factor that could help or hinder one's decision to migrate; 25% of the remaining households ranked these concerns as the second most important factor. Other factors that informants ranked as impediments to migration were, first, a fear of the border and the risks of crossing into the United States (ranked as most important by half of the informants) and, second, the age of the migrant. Migrants were ideally younger, not older, men. The costs of migration and the limits that a job might place on a potential migrant were also considered important.

In contrast, the protests of one's parents ranked lower. Only 17% thought that parents' concerns were the most important factor that might block their decision, 21% said they were of secondary importance, and 21% had no opinion concerning their parents' role in migration decisions. The remaining informants responded that the opinions of their parents had little or no bearing on their decisions. Other factors that might impede migration, but were less important to our informants, included a migrant's health and gender (women should not migrate as much as men), but opinions about these factors were more varied. Finally, the needs of a community did not factor as a very important impediment.

The nature of the social relationships that we found among most migrants, linking them through kinship and friendship with migrants already settled in a receiving community, confirmed the importance of those relationships. We found that of the 275 households that included migrants traveling to internal or international destinations, 64% (or 177) described themselves as having close friends or relatives who were migrants. Only 25% said they lacked any connection to other migrants when their first members left for an internal or international destination.

When we asked migrants to describe their sojourns, 60% of U.S.-bound migrants (70 of 118) mentioned the important role that an already established relative played in making their decision as to their destination. These connections proved slightly more important for women than men. We also found that 89% of the nonmigrating households lacked familial ties to current migrants or a strong friendship with an experienced migrant.

To understand the relationship of migrant to nonmigrant households in the central valleys, we need to look beyond macroeconomic issues, such as the push and pull of labor markets, to various kinds of local assets that migrant and nonmigrant households can bring to bear on their decision-making process (see Faist 1997 and Fischer et al. 1997, 77). Local assets included the following resources: sociodemographic (education, household networks, family status, age of members); economic (work and careers, savings); cultural (the values and practices that inform decision making); environmental and geographic (natural resources and access to them); and community based. None of these assets is shared equally among a community's households. Thus we need also to return to the issue of social inequality and how a lack of access to wealth and power can limit migration for households, while local success makes migration pointless for others.

By the start of the twenty-first century, 62% of San Juan Guelavia's households had a least one member with internal or international migration experience. In contrast, in San Juan del Estado, about 45% of households had sent migrants to national or international destinations, and in Guadalupe Etla only 30% of households included migrants. To understand why anywhere from 40% to 70% community's households opted to stay home even with the allure of good wages and plentiful work in the United

States, I focus on the assets that three nonmigrating households bring to their decision making. The first example is a nonmigrating, marginal household from San Juan del Estado. This example is contrasted with an average nonmigrating household from San Juan Guelavia, and a successful nonmigrant household in Guadalupe Etla.

I classify the San Juan del Estado household as marginal because it lacks land and has no wage laborers and therefore no regular sources of income. Its members hold few kin or communal ties (the heads do not act as godparents, for example), they hold low-status positions in the local *cargo* system, and the male household head uses labor to cover communal expenses that would typically be met through monetary contributions. The second household, from San Juan Guelavia, is characterized as average because it holds some land (about a hectare), and its members combine farmwork with wage labor to cover expenses. The household is embedded in kin and community networks, and its members hold minor positions in various civil *cargos* and act as *compadrazgos* for a few families. Like most households, this one is able to cover its daily expenses with limited savings. There is usually some money to make the occasional luxury purchase, although it is also possible that a crisis will sap resources and stress support networks. I describe the household from Guadalupe Etla as successful because it holds substantial high-quality land and includes a number of wage earners employed in various fields. Furthermore, the household uses its place in kin and communal social networks (particularly the *cargo* system and the sponsorship of godchildren) to increase and earn status within the community.

In San Juan del Estado, I interviewed the Martínez household as one of several follow-ups to surveys in the community. This household could not migrate and existed on the margins of the growing market system that characterized rural life in the village. The household included Don Marco, Doña Flor, Inés (Flor's mother), and two young children. Poor health forced Inés to settle with her daughter and son-in-law after having spent nearly two decades in Mexico City working as a live-in domestic. Her experience in Mexico City brought no resources to Marco and Flor's household. Rather, Inés was now a burden on the household because of her health.

The resources available to the household were limited. The household owned no land, and Marco farmed a quarter of a hectare of wetlands (not irrigated land but land with a high water table) *por la mitad.* Flor took in laundry and ironing, earning about 50 pesos a week for her efforts. Inés brought no savings to the household and did not work. She owned a sewing machine, however, and when she felt well, she took in minor work repairing clothing. Marco and Flor's daughters (ages four and six) were too young to effectively add any labor to the household. Both were in school full-time.

I asked Marco, Flor, and Inés to describe their expenses for me. Marco replied, "Expenses? How can you have expenses if you don't have an income? We do not have any money. We have to ask for help, and God willing, we make it. But we really don't have anything." He added, "My mother-in-law, she used to live away, but now we are taking care of her. She needs medicine, but we can't buy it, and here she is a widow—who will take care of her? Really, we just don't have anything." When I asked the couple how they covered the village's bimonthly charges for water and electricity, Marco answered, "I do extra *tequio*—I trade my service in the community to cover that. But sometimes the electricity is shut off because we can't pay for it. Other times we borrow money to pay—maybe 50 pesos, but I usually trade my time." The situation was the same for water service: "When we cannot pay for water, I go to the river [below the house] and carry buckets for cooking."[3]

Trading labor to cover the costs of utilities is not a bad short-term solution. However, it does carry social consequences. Much of a household's social status and community standing is defined by its members' participation in local social institutions. These include participating in the system of *cargos,* paying *cooperación,* and performing regular service in *tequio.* Using *tequio* to cover weekly or monthly costs removes the reciprocal basis of its original social contract and emphasizes the economic marginality of Marco's household. Thus, one outcome of Marco's actions is to increase the asymmetry that separates marginal and successful households in terms of wealth, status, and standing in the community.

A lack of resources also means that households in marginal positions will hold only low-status positions in low-status *cargos* and *comites.* For Marco this has meant a series of positions as a *topil* (a person who provides informal security for the town) or a *vocal* (a voting member with no leadership) on a minor committee, the *casa de salud* (health clinic).

Later in the survey, I asked Marco, Flor, and Inés to talk a little about migration. Marco responded, "How can we afford to migrate? I have my children to feed; I have my wife and my mother-in-law. I can't leave them alone. Even if I did, where would I get the money to get across the border? Who would help me? Where would I live? I can't do it. I don't even think about it."

Inés talked about her time in Mexico City. She had worked as a servant for a family in the district, earning a very low wage, none of which she was able to save. "I went when my poor husband died," she related. "I had nothing to do and I was very young, so I left my daughter [Flor] with my mother and I went to Mexico City. I spent twenty years there. Can you imagine? Twenty years working my fingers to the bone, and now what have I to show for my time? A sewing machine and bad health!"

The lack of able-bodied workers in marginal households like this one can limit potential income, wealth, and status throughout periods in the developmental cycle of domestic groups. However, we should not assume that marginal households grow out of their predicament as their children mature and become effective workers.

The challenges facing marginal households cannot be explained by using a Chayanovian crisis model, in which problems are solved as the worker-to-consumer ratio improves.[4] Rather, the situation is one in which the marginal household lacks assets (social, cultural, economic, and political) and will have few if any opportunities to gain additional assets to respond effectively to anything more than daily maintenance (Durrenburger and Tannenbaum 2002).

The situation that marginal households like Marco and Flor's face every day—a struggle to put food on the table and to maintain a modest home—pertains to about 18% of the nonmigrating households we surveyed. These households have few resources (that is, they lack land, own few consumer goods, and have few linkages to other households as defined by kin and *compadrazgo* ties), and they often face crises at home (usually a death, an accident, or, as in Inés's case, a medical crisis) that quickly consume any resources and stress network supports.

However, the majority of nonmigrant households (about 58% of the households surveyed) own land and fill wage jobs that provide the money needed to purchase goods and services that members want. They maintain social ties with other households that effectively establish them in local and sometimes regional, national, and transnational flows. For a few households these connections become the basis for successful economic growth and for earning local status and prestige.

San Juan Guelavia is a town that looks as though it has seen better times. Most of the streets are unpaved and there are few satellite dishes and even fewer cars in the town. San Juan Guelavia was once home to salt producers and basket makers who traded their goods throughout the valleys using the local rail line that passed through the community, linking it with Oaxaca City and Tlacolula (Mendieta y Núñez 1960). Today no salt is produced, and basket making is in steep decline. One basket maker commented, "It just isn't worth it. You have to find *carrizo* [reed]. It doesn't grow here any-

Vendor in Tlacolula, May 2002. Photograph by Margaret Fox; reproduced with permission.

more; we don't have enough water. And *carrizo* costs a lot of money. No one buys the baskets either. Before, we would export even to Arizona, but not now."

There is arable land in the community, but it is largely unirrigated. Townspeople regularly told us that Guelavia suffers from a lack of usable resources (see Mendieta y Núñez 1960, 279–280) and, because of increased migration, a lack of skilled workers. It is interesting that Mendieta y Núñez (1960, 321) found little migration as recently as 1957, when he conducted his study. He noted that young men and women traveled occasionally to Oaxaca City to work as domestics or to seek additional education.

Even though migration is common in San Juan Guelavia, not everyone elects to migrate. Some cannot, for reasons similar to those noted in the example of Marco and Flor's household. For others, the decision to stay at home is made carefully and is balanced against what are perceived as the costs and risks of migration.

Amador Méndez, who is fifty-eight years of age, heads an extended household that is typical of nonmigrating households in the community. It includes eight other individuals: Amador's wife, Consuela; their son, Cornelio (age twenty-seven); their daughters Lupe (twenty-two), Rosa (twenty), and Antonia (nineteen); Cornelio's wife, María (twenty-six); and Cornelio and María's two young children. The family farms a hectare of temporal land and grows assorted vegetables and enough maize to cover about a fourth of their yearly demand for tortillas. Money comes from raising animals and renting *yuntas.* Amador described the situation: "I can recover my costs for the house and expenses by raising and selling cows, pigs, *yuntas,* sheep, and goats. I use some of our corn to fatten my pigs, and then I take them to Tlacolula to sell. Every year I take [two teams of] *yuntas* to sell in Tlacolula. I sell them and buy new *yuntas* to train. With my son I rent out my team—I can earn maybe 300 pesos a week [during the planting season], 300 pesos!"

Amador and Cornelio also work irregularly as day laborers in town, building homes and additions. Occasionally Cornelio will travel to Oaxaca if he hears about potential work on a building site. This work can earn up to about 60 pesos per day. Lupe and Rosa work in Oaxaca, where they have jobs as domestics. They are each paid 200 pesos a week plus room and board (see Howell 1999). They travel to Guelavia to spend their days off and to bring their salaries to their mother, who keeps track of the household's assets. Antonia travels to study accounting in Oaxaca City and helps Consuela and María with housework.

When I asked Amador if he would think about migrating, he answered, "I cannot afford it. I don't know who to talk to, and where would I go?" He described the border and migration to the United States in negative terms. He did not object to the process, but he was not sure of the outcome: "My father was one of the first people to go to the States. He went in 1943 as a bracero. But to work now, you need a *patrón,* you need papers. It is a way to earn a lot of money, but it is hard. I see what happens. People leave and they don't want to come back, or they want to change everything. . . . I would rather see jobs come here and not suffer like those poor souls that cross, only to be treated badly." Amador, Consuela, and their household have the resources to carefully weigh the risks of migration and what they see as questionable success against the guarantee of low but steady wage labor. The issue is not one of whether there is money to cover the costs of migration, for in fact there is. Rather the issue is whether risking that money makes sense.

Although the household continues to pool its resources and manage its affairs with enough money to cover daily expenses, some entertainment, and the occasional luxury item, there is little reason to migrate. If Cornelio and María decide to establish an independent home, the balance may shift. Particularly for Cornelio, migration to the United States might become an important alternative. A second factor that adds to Amador's status—and therefore increases the assets and resources the household can turn to in times of stress and crisis—is his continued service to the community through *tequio, cooperación,* fulfilling *cargos,* and family's sponsorship of a *mayordomía* in 1991.

The third example comes from Guadalupe Etla, a town that shares many qualities with San Juan del Estado. Most of the streets are paved, there is a booming local market system, and Oaxacans who are relocating from the city have started a small land boom in the area. We interviewed two families who were in the process of selling land they had gained during agrarian reform in Guadalupe Etla (see DeWalt et al. 1994). Farming and dairy production are important in Guadalupe Etla. The twenty households that reported keeping dairy cattle averaged four cows and earned up to 500 pesos a week.

In Guadalupe Etla, I encountered a household that was able to use its strengths to climb the local status ladder, as well as to carve out a niche for itself in the growing market system that links Guadalupe to Oaxaca City and beyond. Carlos Pérez (age fifty-three) and Virginia Cano (age fifty-one) live with their two sons, twenty-five-year-old Miguel and seventeen-year-old Guadalupe, and their two daughters, fifteen-year-old María and twenty-year-old Carolina. Virginia's mother, Soledad (age sixty-seven), also has lived in the household since her husband died some years ago. The household pools its resources not only to maintain itself but also to invest in higher education and business. Don Carlos divides his time between fieldwork (his irrigated plot produces about a year's worth maize for the family, in addition to some alfalfa, beans, and squash) and renting his 3.5-ton truck for deliveries. Carlos earns a minimum of 150 pesos per delivery and manages between six and ten deliveries a week. This situation is far different for Carlos from the one he knew as a child:

> We used to be so poor in this town [Guadalupe Etla], we didn't even have shoes, and we used our harvest to feed ourselves. . . . But my poor, departed father, he suffered for me and my sisters—he was never satisfied with his life, and he suffered. He would go to Etla to work or to buy and sell goods. He would make a few pesos, a few centavos, but he would take the extra harvest and sell it in Etla or he would take firewood to sell. He saved for us, and when I was old enough, I was able to help him . . . the way my son [Miguel] helps me. It is correct—he helps his papa.

Miguel and his brother, Guadalupe, both work with Carlos in the field and as assistants with the truck rentals. Virginia is occupied with the household but also earns a small income as a seamstress. In the house, her mother lends a helping hand, as do María and Carolina. Miguel's wife, Susanna, lives with him in the household and contributes by helping Virginia with housework and occasional sewing. María and Guadalupe attend the Instituto Tecnológico de Oaxaca, where each pursues a bachelor's degree in business. Guadalupe says, "It was my mom's idea for me to go . . . but I like it. I want to earn my degree and then find a job in Oaxaca [City], maybe working for a delivery service." María has no definite plans yet for her future but has hopes to be a store manager. When she is not in school, she works in a *papelería* and brings her salary back to the household.

No members of the household have ventured farther than Oaxaca City in search of work. When asked about migration, Carlos stated: "Well, over the last years it has really grown, but it isn't something I would recommend. . . . What if you go away for five years? Your wife will suffer for you, and your children won't be satisfied with what they have. In my opinion, migration is not worth the time or suffering. . . . And the obligations you have to the community? You have to pay for that! And what about food? What about the *cargos?* It isn't worth it, not for me."

Carlos and Virginia have invested time and effort supporting the community. Carlos has served on a series of committees, and Virginia has worked in LICONSA. The couple also contributes *cooperación* and gives *tequio* as necessary to community projects and programs regularly. Their sons have served as *topiles.*

In the last year, Carlos was asked to serve as the head of a minor committee (for electricity). For the first time, Carlos declined to serve on a committee and instead paid 5,000 pesos (about US$500) for a substitute to take his place. He will still get credit for the position; however, he is free to pursue his growing delivery business.[5]

Carlos's use of money to cover the social costs of *cargo* service contrasts clearly with Marco's use of labor to meet household expenses in his marginal situation. However, where Marco's labor takes the place of the money he should use to cover expenses, Carlos is able to use his savings to gain more time and create opportunities to earn more money. In each case, the trade emphasizes socioeconomic asymmetries that are growing in what are traditionally based and socially sanctioned reciprocal acts.

Given the examples above, immobility is perhaps not the best term to describe the ways in which "stay-at-homes" and nonmigrating households respond to their situations. Although the majority of these households have not yet seen members travel to other parts of Mexico or the United States, they are active households, struggling and often succeeding in their quest to secure a livelihood.

Many stay-at-homes are involved in local circuits to Oaxaca City. Thus, although migration may not be present in these households, they are not immobile. Many locals depend on these circuits to survive, and they will travel regularly to other communities and the city for education, work, health care, and on rare occasions entertainment (though this is of extremely minor importance), even as they describe international migration in risky terms.

Circuit movers fall into one of three classes: students who travel to Oaxaca City for education; workers in the formal labor force of the city; and campesinos and unskilled workers who travel to Oaxaca to sell produce or crafts or to find occasional work as day laborers. People moving between rural towns and the city are evenly divided between men and women.

In our study, men constituted 75% of the professional workers who traveled between rural towns and Oaxaca City and held jobs in politics and management. Nevertheless, professional women—office workers, teachers, and workers in the health and allied health fields—outnumbered professional men in our total count (29 women, 13 men). Students commuting to Oaxaca were more evenly divided.

Rural Oaxacans also travel regularly to Oaxaca City to find work in the informal labor market. Men seek out construction jobs (like Amador and Cornelio above), and women often find domestic positions. Women and men also travel to Oaxaca to sell goods. The experiences of women in San Pedro Ixtlahuaca who travel the short distance to Oaxaca City to sell tortillas are typical. This kind of work by women is important to households and, combined with the efforts of husbands and sons, supports the household and can effectively limit the need to migrate.

One factor in the different rates of migration in the central valleys is access to labor markets—whether formal or informal—locally and in Oaxaca City. Locals understand that wages are much higher in the United States. However, for those households that can earn enough locally, the option to migrate may not seem important. Ramón González, of Guadalupe Etla suggested, "I know that you can earn 6 dollars an hour for minimum wage—that is like 60 pesos an hour! But if you spend a million pesos to get to the United States to buy something, what is the point? It isn't a good deal."

In 1993 and 1996, migrants and nonmigrants in Santa Ana del Valle described the process of border crossing in innocuous terms. They did not dwell on the risks or dangers of crossing into the United States. Sergio Bautista described his situation: "I go to Tijuana by bus, and I'll call my brother Eloy. . . . He has a green card. He'll come get me in his car and take me up to Santa Monica." Once in Santa Monica, Sergio slides into a job he has held off and on for several years, as a busboy in a Chinese restaurant.

By the year 2000, migration was a much more tense subject. The costs of crossing the border were high, as were the risks. Many households, both migrant and nonmigrant, said that a crossing could easily cost thousands of dollars. For marginal nonmigrants the opportunity to find wage work in the United States had greatly declined. Even some migrants agreed that the situation had changed. Señor Méndez, a former migrant to the United States now living at home in San Martín Tilcajete, stated in January 2002, "Parents see the news, and they know what is going on. They won't let their children migrate." A second informant, Señor Jiménez, also from San Martín, echoed this point, adding, "You have to sell everything to get across the border. If I went, I would have to work just to pay for my trip."

Migrants, though not fully aware of the costs and risks on the border, talked about those risks, and as noted above, at least half of the informants mentioned the dangers they perceive on the border as one reason they might not migrate. In informal conversations Oaxacans talked about border troubles, and most could recall the numbers of Mexicans who had died in the last year as they struggled across the border. Though households with migrant experience were more likely to say they would still seek work in the United States, nonmigrant households appeared to weigh carefully the risks involved in migration to the United States. Thus a second factor that may lead to an increase in the numbers of nonmigrant Oaxacans in these central valley communities is the fear surrounding perceived risks (whether real or not) of migration. This factor is difficult to quantify, but we can note a tendency among nonmigrants in particular to describe migration in increasingly risky terms.

While access to Oaxaca City and its resources and fear of the border are important factors in defining migration outcomes, the most important influences remain the kinship and friendship networks that potential migrants can access and the local assets (whether economic or social) that individual households can bring to bear in daily life. Central to the ability of a household to survive and prosper are the economic assets that are available to its members. These include both fixed assets (such as land) and flexible assets (such as animals and skills) and range from the economic to the social, the geographic to the community-based (Conway 2000; Conway and Cohen 1998; Fischer et al. 1997; Wiest 1973).

Fixed and flexible resources include land, homes, stores, automobiles, and other big-ticket items that can be expensive to buy or build but can sometimes be sold (land, animals) or used to enhance economic standing and status. Households with larger landholdings tend to dominate local affairs. Their reach extends first through contracts they maintain with land-poor households that farm *por la mitad* but also through their domination of local affairs through the service of their members on high-ranking *cargos* and *comites.*

Households also manipulate flexible costs and assets such as labor, education, health care, and leisure time. Health care is a flexible resource, and a household's members can choose either to cover those costs (as Marco and Flor do with Inés) or to minimize costs and hope that crises can be avoided. Leisure time can become an important resource for households as well. Participation in cultural programs in a community (such as the *casas de la cultura* that are found in San Martín Tilcajete, Santa Ana del Valle, and Villa Díaz Ordaz) is one way to gain internal status and standing, but participation in these extracurricular activities can also create opportunities for households to connect with regional and state leaders. In Santa Ana, for example, supporters of the town's museum have gained access to special funds through state programs and an NGO affiliated with the museum. One leader received a truck to haul textiles from Santa Ana del Valle and Villa Díaz Ordaz to Oaxaca City. In addition, he now has a vehicle while the majority of his neighbors must still rely upon bus service.

For marginal households there may be few real assets available to members for investment or even as hedges against potential risks. On the other hand, many rural households (as the example of Carlos and Virginia illustrates) are able to use their wealth effectively to enhance their standing and status. Certainly one of the challenges for anthropology is to follow how households continue to deploy their resources, how those resources change over time, and how migration can influence the strategic use of those resources.

Understanding the networks that migrants access as they move internally and to the United States remains the most critical area for study. Migrants depend on social networks (either familial or communal) as they travel across the border, look for work, and settle into communities throughout the United States. Migrants turn to other migrants already settled in U.S. communities, their families, godparents, and village leaders for monetary support to move across the border. Typically migrants borrow money from these individuals and use their early months in their new homes to pay off their debts. Once in a new setting, nearly all of the migrants we interviewed stayed with relatives (brothers, cousins, fathers) or friends from their hometown, as Massey (1990) found for Mexican migrants in general.

Social networks are established within families and between households. They are amplified through kin and non-kin ties, communal labor, service, and support of village projects and programs (Cohen 1999; Mutersbaugh 2002; Nader 1990). Thus households that lack the network ties and the resources necessary to create more ties through participation are at a severe disadvantage. These limits do not simply affect migration outcomes (or the decision not to migrate) but also, as was pointed out in the examples above, set the stage for future development and growth that can make it quite hard for marginal households to move out of their position.

Finally, there are the intangible cultural beliefs that influence all outcomes. In an earlier work (Cohen 2002), I asked, why do Oaxacans care about their communities? My point was that Oaxacan migrants would likely be expected to turn their backs on hometowns and families, given the burdens that households place upon migrating members. It is also important to remember that at home in Oaxaca, migrants are participants, not criminals; they are fathers and mothers, not "illegals." Local values and rules of participation, while burdensome, also confirm membership and status that fly in the face of the image of the poor migrant in North America. For nonmigrants, codes of conduct and participation are similarly strong and are a resource that households and their members (and communities) can use as they navigate the alienating world of global capitalism.

It is easy to ignore the dynamics of migration in rural Oaxaca and to argue that everyone is leaving. Obviously that is not the case, even as the majority of communities in the state continue to lose their population at a high rate (DIGEPO 1999; Embriz 1993). Nevertheless, migration is not inevitable, and it is not the only solution for local households. What I have shown here are the ways in which three different kinds of households use local assets, circuit moves, agricultural labor, and local opportunities to meet the challenges of their changing economies. I have noted that marginal households are at a disadvantage and that their marginality may increase as economic changes take place, even as typical and successful household manage their situations quite effectively. What remains is to understand the trajectories of these households over the near term and the long term.

Will nonmigrant households send migrants in the future? Most theories argue that the costs of migration drop over time and thus allow for a more diverse pool of individuals to join the migration stream (Massey 1990). This process is critical for individuals who would like to migrate but cannot, because they lack the resources necessary to cross the border. However, the costs of migration, particularly of crossing the border to the United States, appear to be climbing. Two outcomes appear on the horizon. First, tensions on the border and the rising costs of crossing into the United States combine with economic slowdowns in Mexico and the United States to limit the potential pool of migrants who can leave rural Oaxaca. Second, for those Oaxacans who can leave, their return is far less certain. Many migrants—on both sides of the U.S.-Mexican border—mentioned that they were staying in the United States longer than they had originally planned. They said the costs of crossing were too high, so they needed to work longer to break even. More importantly, they feared capture and detention as they returned home. Therefore they elect to stay in the United States rather than return to Oaxaca. Concerning the issue of transnationalism that was raised earlier, we can argue, yes, Oaxacans are following transnational paths as they cross the border—they are even "acting transnational" in the United States. In other words, they are accessing resources through ties of kinship and friendship. Nevertheless, the situation remains problematic at best. Migrant networks tend to bypass nonmigrant households, and the differences separating the two groups appear to be widening. Finally, even as they "act transnational" and follow transnational circuits, migrants from the central valleys remain largely at the mercy of economic forces that are well beyond their control.

Conclusion MIGRATION IN OAXACA'S CENTRAL VALLEYS AND ANTHROPOLOGY

You know, I'd like to see my children play more fútbol.
PATRICIA MELCHOR, SAN MARTÍN TILCAJETE,
JANUARY 2002

Understanding Oaxacan migration is not easy. The variability that exists between communities and the diversity that characterizes area households make this process extremely hard to pin down. Add in the human dimension—that people are unpredictable and that we never act with perfect knowledge—and the goal of understanding migration can seem daunting indeed.

There are moments when our informants let us know just how odd our questions and concerns can be. When I interviewed Patricia Melchor in her home in San Martín Tilcajete in January 2002, we spent about an hour working together on my consensus survey that asked her to rank-order various questions concerning migration and remittance practices. At the end of the interview, as with all interviews, I asked Doña Paty if she had anything that she would like to add to our discussion and interview. She commented on *fútbol,* and we spent another quarter of an hour talking about how parents can keep their children happy and healthy. I had not anticipated a discussion of *fútbol* or of the pros and cons of organized sports for children. Nevertheless, the moment was telling. It is difficult to remember that the topics on which we focus our efforts are not always the topics that concern our informants. Sometimes when our informants bring up the odd topic, like *fútbol,* it's a good thing.

Patricia reminded me that rural Oaxacans from the central valleys have other concerns besides the impact of migration and remittance practices. Her comments referenced the kinds of topics that many informants will easily focus upon if given the opportunity. In a sense, Patricia's concern for her children was the issue that most Oaxacans wanted to talk about, and

Graduation performance, Santa María Guelacé, June 2000. Author photo.

certainly the topic came up regularly as our informants talked about their decisions to migrate, the impacts of migration upon households, and the impact of remittances practices and movement for communities at large. I do not want to overstate the importance of Patricia's commentary, but her thoughts on the need to plan for children and to involve them in the life of their community stand in contrast to the images of migration and migrants with which I started my analysis.

Unlike the Mexican migrant who is a loner, focused on self, and uninterested or unable to think about households and communities, the Oaxacan migrant thinks about his or her family and is deeply concerned for the future and the changes that are ongoing in the region. Nevertheless, this concern is not some kind of essentialistic reaction that is rooted in traditional practices and geography. Rather, Patricia Melchor and the other men and women I talked to over the last several years, both migrants and nonmigrants, remind us that Oaxacans are mothers, fathers, sons, and daughters who are trying the best they can to make the best of the hand they were dealt. Perhaps this is the most important lesson we can take from the analysis of migration and remittance practices in Oaxaca's central valleys.

In this conclusion, I want to do three things. First, I want to summarize the argument and point out where I believe we need to better focus our efforts. Second, I want to argue that relying upon either a "Norteño" model or a traditional, geographically centered approach to illustrate the process and patterns of Mexican-U.S. migration misrepresents how Oaxacans and, I would suggest, most rural Mexicans frame their decisions. We are better served by the idea that a culture of migration is at work. A cultural model of migration moves the issue of migration away from an emphasis on the individual and the often negative characterization of the individual and toward an emphasis on how migrants act as members of households and communities and how those households and communities make sense and order of migration outcomes. Third, I want to suggest that anthropology is positioned among the social sciences to help advance migration studies, largely because anthropologists are able to focus on the social foundation and cultural nature of the moves people make.

MIGRATION IN THE CENTRAL VALLEYS: PROCESSES AND POSSIBILITIES

Rural Oaxacans approach the decision to migrate as one that is rooted in the interests and abilities of the individual, the needs and resources of the household, and, to a lesser degree, the resources of the community. The decision is framed by local and regional economic processes, the market for labor in the area, and the perceived promise of work in the United States or another part of Mexico. A migrant weighs self-interest and ability against and in relation to his or her household's interests and needs, history of movement, and access to resources that will support a move. The majority of migrants come to a decision that reflects their desires—and the desires of the household—to improve or at least maintain its station in life. However, the desires of the individual and the household do not necessarily connect. Rather, in most of the cases of migration we studied, the needs of the household were at least a consideration in the decision to migrate. For the individual, the decision to migrate is framed by a desire to find a job that will pay wages that cannot be found locally. The outcome for the household is that the migrant helps the household cover expenses, secure a future, construct or renovate a home, and receive education. Somewhat surprisingly, an individual's desire to have an adventure was not important to the decision.[1]

Our study has shown that Oaxacans are not abandoning their hometowns. The availability of work in Oaxaca City and the increasing ease with which Oaxacans living in the central valleys can access the city's labor market are two important variables that have limited some of the pull that central valley households feel from the promise of higher wages in

Fiesta in Guadalupe Etla, July 2000. Author photo.

the United States. For other households, the resources that are present at home (whether they be land, skilled craft production within the family, or community-based support) mitigate the need to seek work elsewhere.

Like nonmigrant households, migrant households also remain largely focused on the local; they showed similar levels of community involvement and participation. In spite of the many critical comments we heard concerning migration, we saw very little evidence that migration was a cause of perceived declines in traditional cultural practices.

When migration is the choice—and for a little less than half of the central valley households the decision is typically to migrate—a second decision must be made: is the destination within Mexico, or is it the United States? The majority of central valley migrants decide to cross the border and seek a job in the service industry of Southern California.

Decisions concerning destinations are informed by the social networks the migrant holds and that facilitate movement. Regardless of the resources a household controls, most Oaxacans rely on ties of kinship and friendship to identify destinations, to find a place to live, and to find a job. The few migrants who lack these supports must depend on personal savings and perhaps some luck, for they cross the border at a much greater risk.

One sign that migration has begun to mature—in other words, the migrant pool has grown more diverse—is that the number of migrants moving across the border without social networks has increased somewhat over time. This would suggest that the risks of migration are decreasing. However, this change was tempered by the events of September 11, 2001; the declining U.S. economy; and the sense among many migrants and potential migrants that the dangers and risks of crossing the border were increasing.

We measured the outcomes of migration in the central valleys by exploring the ways in which migrant households use their remittances. We found that most migrants return at least a little something home and that only a minority does not remit. The reach of the household and the weight of family values that are based on cooperation remain strong motivating forces for most migrants. Most migrants remit to support their households, construct and renovate their homes, and pay for education, small purchases, and health care.

A smaller group also remits to support investment, and here we found that rural Oaxacans used remittances to open businesses, buy land, and purchase agricultural implements, as well as animals. These investments are made against an economic backdrop that is marginal at best. The marginality of the local economies in rural Mexico is likely the largest obstacle to growth and development for these communities. In other words, as central valley communities plan for their futures, they must contend both with neoliberal economic policies that cannot solve local problems and with local infrastructures that are substandard and demand far more investment and attention than any local or federal program can afford to support. What is surprising is the effort with which central valley communities meet the challenges of local development. In every town, village governments are organizing projects to extend electrical grids, pave roads, improve access to water, and install sewer systems. Migrants are crucial to these programs. Often they send the money that covers the *cooperación* collected for the projects. Just as important is the training that they receive by working in construction in the United States.

One of the problems that arise from migration and remittance use is the cost to communities in terms of increasing status differences between migrant and nonmigrant households. Currently, the differences remain small, as is evident in the overall outcomes of migration and remittance patterns chronicled here. Most migrant households do not earn a great deal more than their nonmigrating neighbors do. Migrant households do not use remittances to make purchases or to invest in ways that are exceptionally different from the choices that nonmigrant households make. Nevertheless, even though the differences remain small, they distinguish those poorer, marginal nonmigrant households from other, more successful migrant and nonmigrant households. Furthermore, although there are successful households that do not include migrants, many do, and the differences between poor and wealthy, migrant and nonmigrant, are likely to increase.

These patterns and outcomes suggest that we must continue to pay attention to Oaxacan migration. We must continue to monitor migrants as they cross the border, but just as importantly, we must continue to focus on outcomes in sending communities. Many processes and patterns will only be understood through further, long-term study. Is the migrant pool growing more diverse? Are migrants returning home? Are remittances going to investments as households mature and home construction is completed? Will the differences between migrant and nonmigrant households increase? Again, only long-term research will give us answers. Another question concerns the gender of future migrants. Currently women are more likely to follow local circuits and to migrate nationally, but will that pattern hold? As more men leave, will more women follow? Additionally, Consejo Nacional de Población (CONAPO) estimates that the communities of the central valleys (like most of rural Mexico) will pass through a demographic transition in the next ten to twenty years, with populations peaking, only to begin a steady decline (CONAPO 2000). What role will migration play in this process, and if these declines occur, what will be the outcome?

A CULTURE OF MIGRATION

What I have described throughout this book is a culture of migration. What do I mean by that term? I use the idea of a culture of migration to capture the fact that, for rural Oaxacans, migration is an everyday experience. It is accepted as an effective means to an end—economic well-being. Rural Oaxacans do not think of migration as a silver bullet that will resolve all of the inequities that come with being rural peasants or indigenous people in Mexico. Migration is an option, an option that a household can choose as one potential way in which to earn a living. Some rural Oaxacans that we interviewed would talk about migration in negative terms. "Migration is ruining our town," said the *presidente municipal* in San Juan del Estado. "Our children are doing drugs and joining gangs. They are leaving their families and turning their backs on tradition." However, we were not able to find any evidence of this. Children were not joining gangs, although there was some graffiti around town, and no one suggested even a rumor of drugs. As for tradition, we did not find a decline across the communities in participation in the *cargo* systems. Furthermore, *cooperación* and *tequio* are critical institutions throughout the valleys. The decline in local traditional practices, whether it has started or not, may have little to do with migration. Rather, changes in the Mexican Constitution and the privatization of communal lands may be far more central to change (see Otero 1999).

Calling the patterns and processes in Oaxaca a culture of migration does not mean that the migration system functions in some wonderfully consistent fashion over time. The reality of migration and remittance use is far from consistent, but it is also not so destabilizing as to threaten local practices. What I mean when I describe the situation as a culture of migration is that Oaxacans are able to make sense of migration. Put another way, migration fits into local practices as one of many possible ways in which to maintain and sometimes improve a household. Most migrants and nonmigrants are aware that migration is a choice; it is neither good nor evil in and of itself, although it does have costs and benefits. Most households are able to understand those costs and benefits, and most are able to make the choice to stay or go, to migrate or not, as they see fit. It is a sign of the resilience and ingenuity of most rural Oaxacans that they can cope with the changes, that they can integrate migration into the patterns and processes that define their world, and that they can use remittances to accomplish important goals for their households and communities.

Migration and remittance outcomes are but one piece of a rapidly globalizing, capitalist market system that is changing rural Mexico in profound ways. We cannot overlook the importance of the national government's neoliberal policies or of entertainment, the media, education, and evangelism as forces that may contribute as much or perhaps more to patterns of local change than migration does.

Urban Oaxacans are moving to communities like San Pedro Ixtlahuaca and Guadalupe Etla as they search for a more bucolic and what they perceive to be safer existence. Urban transplants can undermine rural systems of rule and community participation. New settlers in San Pedro Ixtlahuaca are pushing for the establishment of party-based politics in place of *usos y costumbres*. Currently, the locally born populace holds an advantage in votes, and although such changes in politics are not likely to occur soon, they are a source of tension.

Neoliberal policies that favor privatization and the removal of public support programs also threaten local communities. Arizpe (1981) stated that the removal of price subsidies and support programs concerning maize production was integral in the first large wave of internal migration that brought thousands of rural Mexicans to the nation's capital in the 1970s. More recently, Otero (1996, 1999) and Gledhill (1995) asserted that neoliberal policies in Mexico, which tend to monetize local economies and further erode social support programs while privatizing national industries, have forced a new wave of migration, this time to the United States. In these cases, migration is better thought of as a symptom of a much larger problem. A focus on migration that fails to note these changes fails to capture the nature of movement.

That other processes besides migration may lead to change became clear in a conversation I had with a friend in Santa Ana del Valle in 1992. We were talking about families that had joined an evangelical church in the village. The presence of these families in the community was a point of heated debate that continues to occupy villagers to the present day. My friend commented that an *evangélico* (a person who has converted) is much like a migrant who leaves his family; both are losses to their household and to the community. There was, however, one important difference. The migrant is a painful loss that can negatively influence a household's ability to cover its expenses, but it is a pain from afar—the migrant has in effect voted with his feet and left. The *evangélico,* on the other hand, is in the community as a focus for debate and tension. For households and communities that depend upon morality, values, and practices such as familial reciprocity and community service to create a sense of belonging and identity, *evangélicos* may prove far more destabilizing, at least in the short run, than the migrants who leave.

ANTHROPOLOGY AND THE STUDY OF MIGRATION

In a recent essay, Caroline Brettell (2000, 98) characterizes anthropological studies of migration as being "focused less on the broad scope of migration flows than on the articulation between the place whence a migrant originates and the place or places to which he or she goes." Brettell (2000, 107) goes on to say that much of the contemporary effort shifts the analysis away from the individual (where he or she goes) and toward the analysis of migrant networks and, in particular, migrant households. This shift has been particularly fruitful in the analysis of migration in the late twentieth century and the rise of transnational movers, that is, migrants who are able to participate in the social life of their sending and receiving communities (Basch et al. 1994; Massey et al. 1998; Portes et al. 2002).

Much of this work focuses on the ways in which migrants create new opportunities in receiving communities while remaining embedded in local cultural processes in sending villages. Although these studies have important implications for understanding Mexican-U.S. migration, they have spent too little time describing methods and models through which transnational outcomes can be studied. In their rush to understand migrants in their receiving communities, they have failed to capture how local patterns influence these outcomes (Conway 2000). Portes et al. (2002, 279) describe the situation as follows: "Qualitative case studies consistently sample on the dependent variable, that is, they document in detail the characteristics of immigrants involved in transnational activities, but say little about those who are not." This is the challenge for studies of migration. We know a good deal about transnational migrants and where they go; what we do not understand as well are the causes of transnational migration or its outcomes and implications for nonmigrants and the households and communities that migrants leave. Finally, because studies tend to sample on the dependent variable, we lack the ability to explain why the percentages of migrants who are transnational vary from one location to another.

I have argued here that in addition to understanding transnationality among migrants who are in the United States, we must pay attention to local social practices in home communities that, while not necessarily transnational or global in their structure, constitute and are created by the transnational processes we investigate (see Meyer and Geschiere 1999, 5; Mittelman 2000, 58). I believe that there is an order to migration that can be observed ethnographically in sending communities. Focusing on these patterns helps us understand the diversity of moves found in rural communities and the variations that characterize rural households.

The analysis of migration cannot begin with transnational migration and migrants living in the United States. Rather we must start in sending communities, by exploring the variables that are involved in all types of movements—whether they are local circuits that link a rural village to the state's capital, national moves to urban centers like Mexico City and agricultural fields in Sonora and Baja California, or transnational moves to the United States.

A study that begins with transnational migration and emphasizes the qualitative experiences of migrants living in the United States risks obscuring or even excluding social practices that may be critical to understanding local variations in social patterns and outcomes. I maintain that anthropology's strength lies in our ability as anthropologists to understand complex patterns and processes in situ. In a sense, I advocate a return to a traditional kind of ethnography, which recognizes that space and place matter—but with a new conceptualization of space and place that is not constrained by geography. Understanding migration in rural Oaxaca begins by understanding its households and communities. To jump to the United States is to lose that foundation and to miss the profound forces that frame and organize the very processes we hope to explain.

Oaxacan migration is complex and involves men and women who follow local circuits, who are bound for national destinations, and who cross international borders. We cannot understand any single piece of this puzzle without looking at the others. The rapidly changing nature of the U.S.-Mexican border only adds to the complications that face rural Oaxacans. In the early 1990s, when I first started working in the region and first began to think about migration, the movement of Oaxacans to the United States was something of a long-distance commute. Individual migrants came and went, clicking into their households and communities when they were in Oaxaca, and assimilating to a small degree when they were in the United States.[2] But as we have seen, those times are over, and the perceived dangers of the border, whether real or imagined, have a powerful effect upon Oaxacans.

Most tragic are the unanticipated costs of a tense and militarized border. Many of the informants I talked to said that if they were to migrate, they would have to stay in the United States longer than they had originally anticipated. First, the costs of crossing into the United States were rising, to as much as US$5,000. Second, and perhaps more important, Oaxacans were nervous and feared being caught by the U.S. Immigration and Naturalization Service (INS). To build upon a successful border crossing, migrants would need to stay much longer. One migrant reasoned, "Why would I come home if I was in the United States? Why would I risk crossing back into Mexico? If INS catches me, I'm done for. I'll never get papers. It is better just to go and stay." A third factor is that Oaxacans are growing angry about the entire situation. They feel as though both Mexican and INS officials have singled them out for abuse.

Oaxacans understand that they are entering the United States as undocumented aliens. What they have a harder time understanding is why such status should matter when jobs in the United States are available. The negative comments of young men concerning migration and the United States are a shift from the statements of older informants concerning migration. Older men typically described their experiences in largely positive ways. For them, going to the United States for a short contract was an effective means for earning a little extra money to help cover a household's expenses. Young migrants today face extreme pressures at home and as migrants. Although the money a migrant remits may not seem like a lot in real terms, it is critical to the survival of a household. Given the trajectory of the Mexican economy and the continued short-term growth in the young adult population, migration is likely to continue apace and perhaps even to increase. It seems to me that our role as anthropologists should be threefold: to continue to document this process; to understand the local costs and benefits of movement; and where possible, to work with policy makers so that they can better understand the challenges facing rural Mexicans and why migration to the United States remains such an attractive proposition.

Appendix A CHARACTERISTICS OF THE POPULATION BY COMMUNITY

Characteristic	*Guadalupe Etla*	*San Juan del Estado*	*Santa Inés Yatzeche*	*San Pedro Ixtlahuaca*	*San Juan del Río*	*San Juan Guelavia*	*San Lorenzo Albarradas*	*Santa María Guelacé*	*Villa Díaz Ordaz*	*San Martín Tilcajete*	*Total*
Age (household head)											
Male	51.5	49.7	46.4	51.5	50.6	48.5	48.7	51.8	52.3	45.8	49.68
Female	48.4	46.6	43	47.9	45.8	47.5	45.2	50.3	49.9	42.8	46.74
Household size											
Total members	6.3	5.4	6.5	5.8	5	6.2	5.8	6.9	5.2	5.7	5.88
Minors per household (average)	1.7	1.8	2.7	2	1.7	2.3	2.4	2.1	1.7	2.1	2.05
Education											
Household head (average years)	6.8	6.1	4.1	5.6	5.9	5.8	5.8	6.7	6.0	6.7	5.943
Children beyond sixth grade	64%	47%	23%	56%	53%	35%	23%	57%	44%	55%	46%
Language spoken											
Spanish	100%	100%	0%	90%	2%	15%	98%	32%	3%	100%	54%
Zapotec	0%	0%	100%	0%	98%	1%	0%	4%	75%	0%	28%
Bilingual	0%	0%	0%	10%	0%	82%	2%	68%	25%	0%	19%
Migrants per household (average)	2.2	2.2	2.0	2.0	1.3	2.4	2.1	1.6	1.8	2.2	1.97
First year migrant left (any destination)	1962	1956	1964	1989	1985	1941	1970	1982	1977	1930	
First year to Mexico D.F.	1990	1960	1964	NA	1986	1942	1970	1982	1977	1930	1995
Average years spent as internal migrant	3.25	19.75	27	NA	10.5	9.87	50	5.44	NA	10.75	11.2
Average number of internal migrations	2	2	1	NA	2	2	2	1	2	1	2

	Average remittance from an internal migrant = 563 pesos a month for 8 years Average age at first internal migration for women = 21 and for men = 22										
First year to USA	1962	1956	1988	1989	1985	1941	1985	1990	1979	1953	1991
Average years spent as migrant in USA	7	7.13	14	NA	5.5	12.08	15.33	6.2	2.5	6.68	8.81
Average number of migrations to USA	1	2	2	NA	1	2	2	2	2	2	2
	Average remittance from USA = US$731.68 (bimonthly) for 6.5 years Average age at first migration to USA for women = 20 and for men = 21										
Living quarters											
Number of rooms (average)	3.7	2.8	NA	NA	NA	3.3	NA	3.6	2.0	3.4	3.8
People per room (average)	2.4	2.7	NA	NA	NA	3.0	NA	2.6	NA	2.6	2.7
Land											
Average hectares	1.87	1.4	1.3	2.2	1.3	2.5	2.2	2.2	2.6	1.3	1.7
Average months' worth of maize grown	6.1	6.5	6.2	4.0	NA	NA	8.2	NA	7.1	NA	4.4

Note: Percentages are rounded.

Appendix B HOUSEHOLD SURVEY

Transnational Migration, Remittances, and Daily Life in Oaxaca:
Survey Directed to the Head of Household, Summer of 2000, 2001

Town:
Date and time of the interview:
Survey form number:
Name of interviewer:
Information on interviewee:

Block #, Address, Street Name, #, Neighborhood/Section
Draw a map where the house is located (signal: the North, direction in which the municipal palace and some familiar place are found, the name of two streets that circle the block).

Describe the informant (dress, shoes, hairstyle):

Where was the interview carried out?

How was the interview?
☐ excellent ☐ good ☐ easy ☐ normal ☐ difficult ☐ very difficult

Who were other people present?

How well does the person interviewed speak Spanish?
☐ excellent ☐ well ☐ normal ☐ poor ☐ bad

Do you recommend this family for a longer interview? ☐ yes ☐ no

I: THE FAMILY UNIT

List all members of the household by name

Indicate sex of each member __male __female

Indicate relationship of all members with household head:
__Head (f) __Head (m) __spouse
__son/daughter __mother/father __brother/sister
__brother/sister-in-law __grandchild
__father/mother-in-law __other __not related

Indicate age for each member

Indicate marital status for each member
__single __married __cohabiting
__single mother __widowed __divorced

Place of birth of each member (note community)

Educational achievement for each member
__elementary __ninth grade __high school
__college __grad school

Language(s) spoken by members
__Zapotec __Spanish __Zapotec & Spanish
__Mixtec __Mixtec & Spanish
__other (specify)

Indicate if each member of the household lives in the house. If not present in the household, indicate where the member resides.

II: PRODUCTIVE ACTIVITIES OF HOUSEHOLD MEMBERS

For each member of the household indicate
Name
Main activity
The three most important productive activities of each person
Place of work (location, *municipio,* state)

Time in the job

Works for money? __yes __no

Income or earning __hourly __daily __biweekly
(Estimate wages)

Describe what you sell:

Number of days worked per week (1–7)

What percentage of your earnings goes to the household?

How much income do you give to the family for spending?

III: PRESENCE OF MIGRATION

Are there migrants in your family? __yes __no

Do you have family in:
__the city of Oaxaca? (note street, neighborhood)
__other parts of Mexico? (note locality, state)
__the United States? (note locality, state)

How many migrants (people who live and work outside of the house and locality) are there in your family?

Do you know how to migrate to other parts of Mexico? (explain)

Do you know how to migrate to parts of the U.S.? (explain)

Please fill out the following for each migrant and for each migration made:

Migration: __first sojourn __second or more __last time
Name of migrant:
Date of exit:
Destination:
Migration began: (month / year) End: (month / year)
Is the person still away from the community? __yes __no
How much did the trip cost?
How did s/he get the money?
__savings __family money __loan __gift
__land sale __animal sale __other _____

What type of work does s/he realize? Income:
With whom does s/he live there?
__family __countryman __employer __alone __other
Is there a migrants association in the destination community?
__yes __no
How much money did you send or bring back? (explain)
How do you send the remittances?
__Western Union __bank transfer __other wire transfer
__pocket transfer __exchange house __other _____
Remittances are sent:
__monthly __every 6 months __yearly __other _____
How were the remittances used?

IV: AGRICULTURE

Do you own farm land? __yes __no
Describe land:
Dry land ___hectares
  __individual holding __family property __rented
Irrigated ___hectares
  __individual holding __family property __rented
Wet land ___hectares
  __individual holding __family property __rented
This year, did you split your parcels with someone?
__yes __no
  If yes, how did you divide the harvest?
    __by rows __in equal parts __other _____
This year, did you rent any of your parcels?
__yes __no
How much corn does your family consume daily? ___kilos
What crop did you farm this year?
(include types of crops, hectares planted, and months of harvest)
Did you farm (plant and harvest)
Corn __yes __no
Beans __yes __no
Alfalfa __yes __no
Other (specify):
Did you sell your harvest? __yes __no
  If yes, how much did you earn?
Animals—indicate total number of:
Donkeys

Horses
Pigs
Cows
Lambs
Goats
Turkey
Chickens
Other (specify)
How many animals do you have?
Explain value of animals:
How many animals did you sell last year?
Why did you sell them?
Do you have a team of oxen? (value) __yes __no
If yes, do you rent your oxen? __yes __no
Do you own a tractor? (value) __yes __no
If yes, do you rent your tractor? __yes __no
Do you own an oxcart? (value) __yes __no
If yes, do you rent your oxcart? __yes __no
When migrants are away, who is in charge of working your land?
__male sons __intermediary __wife __lent it
__father-in-law __fallowed land __hired help
__the family without the husband __other ______
When your husband or children leave to work outside the community, how do you get the money to farm?

V: EXPENDITURES THAT THE FAMILY UNIT HAS

Approximately how much money did you spend last week?
How much money did you spend last week on:
Utilities (electricity, water, and gas/firewood)
Food (corn, tortillas, meat, vegetables, etc.)
Health
Education
Entertainment
Clothing
Transportation
Other, specify:
Total expenses for a week

Do you have a bank account? __yes __no

VI: HOUSING

Do you _____ your home?
__rent __own __borrow __share
__housesit __other _____ __doesn't know/answer
What year did you acquire or inherit the land for this house?
How did you obtain the money for buying or building this house?
__savings __migration __loan __sold land
__inherit __sold animals __gift _____ other
Did you use *guelaguetza* in building this house? __yes __no
What type of fuel do you use for cooking? (mark all options that apply)
__wood __coal __petroleum __gas __electricity
_____ other
How do you obtain water for domestic use? (mark all options that apply)
__water pipe __public water pipe __public well
__private well __purchase bottled water __other, specify:
Do you treat cooking or drinking water? __yes __no
What treatment? __pills (chlorine) __bleach __boiling
__other, specify:
Do you have:
Bathroom __yes __no
Toilet __yes __no
Septic tank __yes __no
Connection to public sewer __yes __no
How many bedrooms are there in the lot?
How many people sleep per room?
How many floors does your house have?
Mark the main building materials for:
Walls:
__plastic
__carton
__wood
__metal sheets
__*bajareque:* mud/reed
__adobe
__polished wood
__concrete blocks (*tabicón*)
__blocks
__other, specify:
Roof:
__palm, straw, reed
__tile
__carton or zinc sheets

__asbestos sheet
__concrete slabs
__other, specify:
Floor:
__dirt
__wood
__blocks, mud slabs
__raw cement
__finished cement
__mosaic
__other, specify:
Object—number
__electrical/gas water heater
__firewood water heater
__sprinkler
__refrigerator
__gas/electric stove
__washing machine
__manual/pedal sewing machine
__electrical sewing machine
__blender
__electric iron
__bed type (with mattress, not including cribs)
__couch or sofa
__dining table
__tape recorder
__record player
__CD player
__radio (not part of recorder)
__TV
__bicycle
__motorcycle
__truck
__car
__computer
__VCR
__microwave oven
__Nintendo, Play Station, Gameboy
__cable/ satellite dish
__Other, specify:

VII: COMMUNITY PARTICIPATION OF THE FAMILY UNIT

In the last year, has a family member participated in *tequio?*
__yes __no
Do you use substitutes for *tequio?* __yes __no
If you used a substitute, how much did you pay him/her?
Do you have a *guelaguetza* book? __yes __no
Are you godparents? __yes __no
How many godchildren do you have in total? __
How many baptism godchildren do you have? __
Have you sponsored a *mayordomía*/saint's day celebration?
__yes __no
In what year(s)?
Do you pay cooperation to the authorities? __yes __no
When you need help, who do you go to?
__parents __siblings __other relatives
__friends __other people (specify)
In the last year, has any household member served in a *cargo*/commitee?
__ycs __no (explore)
Why are you not fulfilling a *cargo* right now?
__done with *cargos*
__taking a break
__another reason, specify:
Did you use substitutes for the *cargos* that were assigned to you? __yes __no
If you used a substitute, how much did you pay him/her?
Service history for each person in the household, including:
Name of the person
Years of service
List of *cargos*/committees
List of positions in *cargos*/committees

Appendix C CULTURAL CONSENSUS

This survey is designed to obtain a "cultural consensus" concerning migration in your community.

Background information:
Community
Date
Survey given by
Address of household

Describe the household (Take into account the quality and size of the house; presence of furniture, electrical appliances, bathrooms, vehicles, satellite dish; business ownership)
___ poor ___ average ___ rich

Characteristics of the household
    Number of people in the household
    Amount of land the household possesses
    The household has migrants? ___ yes ___ no
    The household has minors? ___ yes ___ no

Rank each option along the following scale:
1 = strongly agree
2 = agree
3 = neutral
4 = disagree
5 = strongly disagree

People migrate
___In search of a job
___To improve the livelihood of the family
___To be able to save

___To be able to buy furniture, appliances, a truck, etc.
___To have an adventure
___Other (specify)

Rank your agreement with the following reasons to migrate
___Daily sustainability of the family
___For lack of jobs
___To build a house
___So their children can go to school
___To participate in parties
___To buy a land, oxen, breeding animals, a truck
___To be able to save
___To be able to pay for family medical bills
___Other

Rank your agreement with the reasons that keep a person from migrating
___Family
___A job
___The town
___Age of the migrant
___Health of the migrant
___That the migrant is a woman
___Parents
___Migration costs
___The dangers of crossing the border and living in the U.S.

Rank typical migrants who go to the U.S.
___Your son
___Your daughter
___Your husband or wife
___You
___A head of family
___A young and single man
___A young and single woman
___A single father
___A single mother

Rank typical migrants who go to other parts of Mexico
___Your son
___Your daughter
___Your husband or wife
___You
___A head of family

___A young and single man
___A young and single woman
___A single father
___A single mother

Rank your agreement with who travels to the city of Oaxaca
___Your son
___Your daughter
___Your husband or wife
___You
___A head of family
___A young and single man
___A young and single woman
___A single father
___A single mother

Rank your agreement with the following reasons to migrate to the U.S.
___Work
___Education
___Entertainment
___Medical services
___Shopping
___Visit relatives
___Other

Rank your agreement with the following reasons to migrate to other parts of Mexico
___Work
___Education
___Entertainment
___Medical services
___Shopping
___Visit relatives
___Other

Rank your agreement with reasons to travel to Oaxaca City
___Work
___Education
___Entertainment
___Medical services
___Shopping
___Visit relatives
___Other

Rank agreement with the following remittance uses
___Daily sustainability of the family
___To create a secure source of work
___Building a house
___Education
___Parties
___Purchase of large items (furniture, appliances, vehicle, pump, etc.)
___Purchase of land (urban or for farming)
___Purchase of work and breeding animals (oxen, cattle, pigs)
___Savings
___Family medical services
___Other

Rate how you have used remittances if applicable
___To buy food
___To buy fertilizers, animal feed, fuel, etc.
___To buy building materials
___To buy work or fattening animals
___To pay for the children's education
___To pay for the family's medical services
___To invest in a business
___Other (specify)

Rate your agreement concerning what you would do if you received remittances
___Would buy food
___Would buy fertilizers, animal feed, fuel, etc.
___Would buy building materials
___Would buy work or fattening animals
___Would pay for the children's education
___Would pay for the family's medical services
___Would invest in a business
___Other

Rate your agreement with the following statement:
Migration is good because
___The money earned helps the families
___The money earned helps the town
___The goods purchased help the sustainability of the family
___You can see the world
___You learn new trades

Rate your agreement with the following statement:
Migration is bad because

___The family loses income
___It destroys families
___Youth join or form gangs *(cholos, grafiteros, rockeros, scualos)*
___Migrants return with illnesses
___The undocumented immigrants live fearful of the *"migra"*
___Brings along delinquency and drug addiction
___Brings other risks

What are typical destinations for migrants from your community?
___To the United States, specify the place
___To other parts of Mexico, specify the place

For the following questions, please select the better option:
Which is better
___Emigrate with papers
___Emigrate without papers

Who is better, a man who
___Is with his family and is poor
___Leaves and earns a lot of money but never sees his children

Who is better, a man who
___Earns little money in his town
___Earns a lot of money in the United States

Who is better, a woman who
___Is at home without money in charge of her family
___Works in the city of Oaxaca

Who is better, a son who
___Works in the field
___Is a migrant

Who is better, a son who
___Is a migrant
___Is in school

Who is better, a son who
___Works for a salary in Oaxaca
___Is a migrant and works in the field in the U.S.

Who is better, a son who
___Is a migrant and lives with relatives

___Is a migrant and lives alone

What is better for migrants?
___Work in the field
___Work in construction
___Work in a restaurant

Which is better?
___A migrant with 1 year of experience in the U.S.
___A migrant with over 3 years of experience in the U.S.
___A migrant with over 10 years of experience in the U.S.

What is better for a migrant?
___Go to the U.S. without the wife and children
___Go to the U.S. with the wife and children
___Go to the U.S. and have a baby

Who is better, a daughter who
___Works as a domestic in Oaxaca
___Is in school
___Is at home

Who is better, a man
___Rich without kids
___Poor with a lot of kids
___Comfortable with 2 or 3 kids

In a few sentences, describe your ideal family:

NOTES

INTRODUCTION

1. Translation mine.

2. Translation mine.

3. Ravenstein (1889) defined the "laws of migration" and argued that economic disparities between countries (for example, differences in wages) were a driving force in migration patterns. For more on this model, see the discussion of segmented labor market theory in Massey et al. (1998, 33).

4. John Watanabe (1992) describes this perspective as "essentialistic." Essentialism defines a population according to the presence or absence of a series of cultural, linguistic, and geographic markers. Thus, essentialist models tend to reify populations and focus on concrete markers of identity (clothing and language, for example) rather than the outcomes of action. In other words, essentialists focus on what people are rather than what people do.

5. INEGI numbers are problematic at best, and questions abound over their accuracy. The estimates of migration are likely low. However, here I am interested in national patterns, and I believe that the totals, though low, are indicative of the relative size of the migrant pool in various states and therefore are reasonable for comparative investigation.

6. The total for the state adds up to more than 100 percent. This anomaly is likely due to multiple moves as described by migrants in their home communities.

7. Laura Nader (1969) makes clear how difficult it is to conduct comparative work in Oaxaca that is based on the concept of ethnic identity. She argues that any approach to the comparative study of Oaxaca must pay attention to economic organization first.

8. The struggle between traditional political systems (*usos y costumbres*) and politics *por partidos* (party based) has increased in recent years. Part of the shift comes from urban migrants who moved into communities like San Pedro Ixtlahuaca and refused to join the *cargo* system. In other communities the parties (PRI, PAN, and PRD) apply direct pressure on the populace to change their systems of rule. In Oaxaca the *cargo* system continues to dominate local politics.

9. An indigenous identity is not the source of poverty in rural Oaxaca. Rather, poverty is a result of the state's neglect and the lack of rural investment that has marked most of Mexico's history.

10. Even though prosperity ruled San Martín Tilcajete in 2000, by the end of 2001 the market had shrunk drastically. The drop in sales, in response to the declining U.S. economy through 2002, has had a heavy impact on craft production throughout the region (see Chibnik 2003, 245–246).

11. The quotations that appear throughout the text are summarized from interviews conducted during fieldwork in 2000 and 2001. The names of individuals have been changed; however, communities are accurately portrayed.

12. It is difficult to estimate the total of annual remittances to Mexico from the United States. Much of the money returned to the country likely follows informal paths, including pocket transfers. The Banco de México estimates that formal transfers totaled approximately US$2 billion in 1990; however, an additional US$4 billion may have been returned through informal transfers, according to TELECOMM-SEPOMEX (Lozano Ascencio 1993, 2). Whatever the total, the effects of the money remitted to Mexico are profound (see Martin 1996).

13. A household is more than a building. It is a domestic unit—those individuals who share food and resources—and can include people in more than one place (such as a California-based migrant who remits to a home in the central valleys). A household is not the same as a family, although most rural Oaxacans live in households that are based in nuclear families. A household includes everyone who participates in shared activities (cooking, cleaning, working) and everyone who shares or pools resources; and it follows a trajectory, or domestic cycle, through time and space (Folbre 1988; Fortes 1971; Netting et al. 1984; Pennartz and Niehof 1999; Royce 1981; Wheelock 1992; Wilk 1989, 1991). Finally, it is important to remember that plenty of people opt out of their household responsibilities (the migrant who "disappears," for example), but understanding these changes at the household level helps us to appreciate why migration can be so costly to a household.

14. Gaining the informed consent of participants is crucial to the success of any project. As researchers, we should be able to explain our work to our informants, and we must respect their wishes if they elect not to participate. The Institutional Review Board at Pennsylvania State University has reviewed and approved this project. We also explained our project to each community's leaders and proceeded only after we had received their permission to conduct our work.

15. Slightly less than 10 percent of the households surveyed include migrants who have left their homes and severed connections. We cannot estimate the number of families who have left their communities en masse; however, village leaders and community members did not mention a problem with families or households disappearing.

CHAPTER 1

1. My estimate of 10 percent may be low, but working with households that included missing migrants does give us the opportunity to define what the loss of a member (or members) means to a household and a community.

2. Similar changes arise within households as children marry, members die, and children are born. However, I will concentrate here on the outcomes, as they are manifested in migration situations.

3. There were significant positive correlations at the .01 confidence level between the variable "total members in household" and (1) "total migrants in the household," (2) "total migrants in Mexico," and (3) "total migrants in the United States." Similarly, correlations were significant at the .01 confidence level for "total migrants in the household" and the age of both the male and female household heads.

4. The Immigration Reform and Control Act of 1986 was signed into law by Ronald Reagan in January 1987. The act allowed for higher rates of legal immigration and the naturalization of millions of undocumented Mexicans living in the United States. At the same time, the act formalized what Massey et al. (1998, 49) have described as "increasingly harsh and repressive policies" that lowered benefits for migrant workers and increased sanctions for employers who hired undocumented migrant workers.

5. Pigs and goats generate a limited income, and they are not often profitable. Rather they are ways to "bank" money. In a period of crisis or when cash is needed, a family can sell its stock animals for a quick infusion of cash. A much more profitable investment is a team of oxen. A team of trained oxen is often worth thousands of dollars.

6. Unfortunately, deficiencies are more typical in the region. On average, seven of every ten years are marked by low yields for maize (Martha Rees, pers. comm.).

7. Mestizos also practice or participate in *guelaguetza*. However, these reciprocal relationships are most often found among native Oaxacans (Acevedo and Restrepo 1991; Murphy and Stepick 1991; Nader 1990).

8. To evaluate the continued importance of cooperative and reciprocal relationships to migrant and nonmigrant households, I modeled the rate of migrant and nonmigrant household participation in community affairs and used a two-tailed *t*-test to determine whether there was a significant difference in the outcomes for the two groups. I scored all households according to whether a member had participated in *tequio* and *cooperación* over the previous year, and the total number of *cargo* positions members recalled holding in their local hierarchy. The first variable, which I called CPTOT (community participation total), combined the presence or absence of *tequio* and *cooperación* in a household. I scored households with a 1 for the presence of a member in the household who contributed *tequio* or 0 when no *tequio* was contributed. Similarly, a score of 1 indicated that the household contributed funds to *cooperación,* whereas a 0 indicated that no funds were contributed. The sec-

ond variable was the total number of *cargo* positions that a household's members held over time, regardless of status. The total number of *cargos* held (TOTCARGO) ranged from 0 (none) to 16.

I assumed that nonmigrant households would outscore migrant households, indicating that migration destabilizes and undermines participation in traditional patterns of association. I used a two-tailed *t*-test with each variable and found no significant difference between migrant and nonmigrant households:

CPTOT: $t = -1.45$, $df = 588$, and $p = .147$
TOTCARGO: $t = -.32$, $df = 384$, $p = .746$

9. One of the powerful myths in Mesoamerica tells us that rural households prefer to have lots of children, because each child is viewed as an able-bodied worker. However, the myth never focuses on the costs of raising those children. In four of the communities we visited, we asked informants to describe the ideal family. Rural campesinos (farmers), as well as professionals with careers, all described the perfect family as one with no more than three children. They typically stated that more than three children were too expensive and a significant burden on a household and its resources.

CHAPTER 2

1. Migrants like Don Mario and Doña Christina do not like breaking laws and overstaying their visas. Nevertheless, they felt that they had few alternatives. They wanted to see their children and meet their new grandchildren, but they could not easily cross the border. The purchase of the tourist visas used savings that were already low because of the couple's commitments at home. Don Mario had little choice, in his words, other than to stay. My sense is that migrants would prefer to move to the United States by following legal routes, but they feel that it is nearly impossible to do so (Heyman 1998).

2. My wife and I lived in Felix's house during our stay, and it has served as a temporary home for anthropologists and others who visit the community.

3. Mountz and Wright (1996) also report strong connections between the village of San Agustín Yatarení and Poughkeepsie, New York.

4. Migration has been a force throughout Oaxaca's history. However, the scope of that history is far more extensive than I can recount in this volume. Following are three examples of what I mean. First, according to the stories we heard in Santa María Guelacé and San Juan Guelavia, the village of Guelacé was founded by Guelavian families who relocated to protect farmlands and rich soils. Second, Santa Ana's origins also lie in local migrations. In this case, itinerant merchants moving through the valleys established a small community at the site of a spring that today serves as Santa Ana's main well (see Cohen 1999). Third, several natives of San Juan

del Estado described the early history of their community as being rooted in the arrival of Nahuatl speakers just before the arrival of the Spanish. For this mestizo town, the stories appear to create a sense of identity that is picturesque rather than mundane. Nevertheless, we were able to find little evidence that Nahuatl speakers ever entered or settled in San Juan del Estado.

5. Foster (1979, 29) noted that nearly half of the men in Tzintzuntzan, Michoacán, traveled to the United States and that many participated in the bracero program. He also stated that the program's demise in 1964 had a negative economic impact on the Mexican community.

6. Currently, a lawsuit brought against the U.S. and Mexican governments and several banks seeks to recover monies that former braceros allege they were never paid. The money in question comes from a part of the bracero program that stipulated 10 percent of any worker's wages would be held back and sent upon completion of a contract to the bracero in question. The class action lawsuit maintains that between $500 million and $1 billion is owed to former bracero workers (Ponce de León 2002).

7. Abraham Iszaevich, working in six central valley communities, notes that although migration to the United States was present, it did not dominate household decision making. For example, regarding Soledad Etla, he states, "Before 1966, I have no doubt that there was literally no migration to the United States" (1988, 191; translation mine). A lack of international movers before the 1960s is confirmed by the stories I have collected in the field, particularly from older informants.

8. Beverly Chiñas (1993) notes a similar pattern among market women living in the Isthmus of Tehuantepec. She describes working with market women who traveled throughout the isthmus but also went to Oaxaca City to sell mangoes, among other things.

9. CONAPO (2000) notes that the populations of nearly every rural town in Oaxaca should begin to decline in the next decade. By 2020, populations for most towns will be at levels not seen since the 1960s and 1970s. Some of this drop will be due to migration and households that are opting to leave rural communities. However, some of the drop will also be a response to changes in expectations about family and the number of children that is "ideal." Anecdotal evidence suggests that rural Oaxacans are becoming proactive—planning their families and having fewer children. Whether this change will translate to less migration (because there will be fewer mouths to feed) or more migration (because the investment per child will be greater—as will the expectations for those children) is one of those questions that anthropology must begin to address.

CHAPTER 3

1. A professional career was the only type of job that limited or reduced the probability that Oaxacans from the central valleys would migrate.

2. Correspondence analysis is a technique that allows for the multidimensional scaling (mapping) of contingency tables, representing both the rows and the columns of a matrix in the same multidimensional space (Greenacre 1984; Weller and Romney 1990). We use correspondence analysis to represent the rows (communities) and the columns (migration outcomes) of table 3.4 in multidimensional space. The contingency tables show the various migration outcomes defined for each community, as well as the grand totals for each outcome. The association, or "correspondence," between communities and outcomes is presented in figure 3.1. Communities that are more similar are closer to each other in the two-dimensional space, and more similar outcomes are closer as well. In addition, communities that exhibit particular outcomes more frequently than others are closer to those outcomes in the space.

3. Migration in San Pablo Huitzo has reached a level of maturity over its history: fewer new migrants have left the village in the last twenty years than might be expected in other central valley communities. Massey et al. (1994) argue that, in such a situation, migration loses some of its momentum as local opportunities increase and the pool of potential migrants shrinks.

4. In 2002, Roman again mentioned his dream. He had made one more trip to the United States in 1997, staying two years. But by 2002 he was content to stay home, build a small library, and enjoy his first grandchildren.

CHAPTER 4

1. Lozano Ascencio (1993) estimated that migrants returned at least $55 million to Oaxaca in 1990.

2. It is important to note that Kearney's recent work (1994) focuses on the ways in which migrants carefully negotiate the divide between their rural homeland and urban receiving cities. The economics of migration have not changed. What has changed is the way in which we approach the subject of migrant decision making.

3. The pessimism that permeates this model is not restricted to Mexico or even to the Western Hemisphere. Researchers have made similar arguments for the American Samoa and the Philippines (McArthur 1979; Shankman 1976), India (Helweg 1983), and Thailand (Mills 1993).

4. Informants ranked each of the responses, using a five-item Likert-type scale: 1 = strongly agree; 2 = agree; 3 = neutral; 4 = disagree; 5 = strongly disagree.

5. We obtained frequencies for ranked items, using the following equation:

$$S = \frac{[\_(1 - R + 1/L)]/L}{N}$$

where R = the average rank of an item and L = the length of the rank list (in this case the five options were as follows: agree strongly, agree, neutral, disagree, disagree strongly).

6. In three cases, informants who were all female household heads grew angry when they read the option "to have an adventure." Each of these informants argued that an adventure was such an extremely inappropriate motive that she wanted to rank it below any option on the Likert scale we had supplied.

7. A household's overall health is also enhanced by home building and improvements. The decline in chronic diseases that comes with home improvements has a direct impact on the resources that a household has available for other kinds of uses.

8. These figures are quite consistent with Lowell and de la Garza's findings (2002, 19) that 60% of migrants in the United States reported remitting about US$260 per month.

9. Migrants and nonmigrants alike were quite aware of the death toll among Mexicans crossing the border. Migrants were also concerned for their safety following the September 11, 2001, attacks on the World Trade Center and the Pentagon. For some, these concerns were more than enough to decide against migrating, but others, worried over the collapse of Oaxaca's tourism industry following the attacks, saw few options other than to cross the border and find work (see Smith and Ellingwood 2001).

10. Additionally, there are few if any local banks in which to place money, and where banks are accessible, interest rates are extremely low.

11. In 2003 an Internet café also opened in Santa Ana del Valle.

12. Although I have a sense that my informants were correct when they told my research team that *cooperación* is more important than it was in the past—a time when *tequio* provided labor to cover what *cooperación* covers at the present—I do not have direct evidence of this change.

13. Solidaridad is a program that was begun under the auspices of the Salinas administration. Through the program, the state matches local funds for rural development projects.

CHAPTER 5

1. Although the rate of household migration from the central valleys amounted to 46% of all households, the range of rates among individual communities varied from a low of 22% of the households in San Pablo Huitzo to a high of 60% in San Juan del Estado. Thus it is important to explain why 54% of the households we surveyed had not yet elected to migrate.

2. Of course, there are poor households that will risk everything to send a migrant across the border. However, these migrants must in effect mortgage their very lives and in some situations become little more than indentured slaves to unscrupulous, unethical, and immoral smugglers and employers (see Nangengast et al. 1992; Runsten and Kearney 1994).

3. Drawing water directly from the river is difficult—during the dry season

the river sometimes ceases to flow. During the rainy season, the water is easily contaminated, for it flows over garbage that covers the banks.

4. Chayanov argued that generally, among peasant households (like many rural Oaxacan households), production is keyed to immediate need and not to profit margins. Peasant economics could be best understood by analyzing the ratio of laborers to consumers in a household and the balance that exists between family needs and the "drudgery" of labor (Thorner et al. 1966, xv).

5. Mutersbaugh (2002) found a very different situation in the Sierra Norte of Oaxaca. In his example, villagers developed sanctions in response to the nonparticipation of locals in *tequio* and the *cargo* system. Sanctions for nonparticipation ranged from fines to expulsion from the community.

CONCLUSION

1. This view comes in part because my study focused on sending households in sending communities. I would imagine that if we were to interview the 25% of all migrants who do not remit, we might hear a different story. However, the point of this study was not to focus on the migrants who disappear or leave their households. Rather, the goal was to understand the impacts of migration for the sending communities and their populations.

2. One migrant described going to the United States in the late 1980s as an opportunity to get healthy. He was not interested in access to United States health care; rather he would "dry out" and not drink during his time as a migrant. He also commented that his diet greatly improved, and his weight would go down. This is not something that he talks about today, even though he has returned twice to the United States since the late 1980s. Now he mentions how tense he is and how dangerous he feels that Southern California has become.

REFERENCES CITED

Acevedo, María Luisa, and I. Restrepo. 1991. *Los valles centrales de Oaxaca.* Oaxaca: Centro de Ecodesarrollo, Gobierno de Oaxaca.

Adelman, Irma, and J. Edward Taylor. 1990. "Is Structural Adjustment with a Human Face Possible? The Case of Mexico." *Journal of Development Studies* 26(3): 387–407. Quoted in Durand et al. 1996a, p. 425.

Adelman, Irma, J. Edward Taylor, and Stephan Vogel. 1988. "Life in a Mexican Village: A SAM Perspective." *Journal of Development Studies* 25: 5–24.

Alarcón, Rafael. 1992. "Norteñización: Self-Perpetuating Migration from a Mexican Town." In *U.S.-Mexico Relations: Labor Market Interdependence,* ed. J. Bustamante, R. Hinojosa, and C. Reynolds, pp. 302–318. Stanford, CA: Stanford University Press.

Arizpe, Lourdes. 1981. "The Rural Exodus in Mexico and Mexican Migration to the United States." *International Migration Review* 15(14): 626–649.

Basch, Linda G., N. G. Shiller, and C. S. Blanc. 1994. *Nations Unbound: Transnational Projects, Postcolonial Predicaments, and Deterritorialized Nation-States.* Amsterdam: Gordon and Breach Science Publishers.

Bernard, H. Russell. 2002. *Research Methods in Anthropology: Qualitative and Quantitative Approaches.* 3rd ed. Walnut Creek, CA: AltaMira Press.

Brana-Shute, Rosemary, and Gary Brana-Shute. 1982. "The Magnitude and Impact of Remittances in the Eastern Caribbean: A Research Note." In *Return Migration and Remittances: Developing a Caribbean Perspective,* ed. W. F. Stinner, K. De Albuquerque, and R. S. Bryce-Laporte, pp. 267–290. RIIES Occasional Papers, no. 3. Washington, DC: Research Institute on Immigration and Ethnic Studies, Smithsonian Institution.

Brettell, Caroline B. 2000. "Theorizing Migration in Anthropology: The Social Construction of Networks, Identities, Communities, and Globalscapes." In *Migration Theory,* ed. C. B. Brettell and J. F. Hollifield, pp. 97–136. New York: Routledge.

Brettell, Caroline B., and James F. Hollifield, eds. 2000. *Migration Theory.* New York: Routledge.

Bustamante, Jorge A., Guillermina Jasso, J. Edward Taylor, and Paz Triqueros Legarreta. 1998. "Characteristics of Migrants: Mexicans in the United States." In *Migration between Mexico and the United States,* vol. 1, pp. 91–162. Austin, TX: Mexican Ministry of Foreign Affairs and the U.S. Commission on Immigration Reform.

Cancian, Frank. 1965. *Economics and Prestige in a Maya Community: The Religious Cargo System in Zinacantan.* Stanford, CA: Stanford University Press.

———. 1990. "The Zinacantan Cargo Waiting Lists as a Reflection of Social, Political, and Economic Changes, 1952–1987." In *Class, Politics, and Popular Religion in Mexico and Central America,* ed. L. Stephen and J. Dow, pp. 63–76. Society for Latin American Anthropology Publication Series, no. 10. Washington, DC: Society for Latin American Anthropology.

Chance, John K. 1990. "Changes in Twentieth-Century Mesoamerican Cargo System." In *Class, Politics, and Popular Religion in Mexico and Central America.* ed. L. Stephen and J. Dow, pp. 27–42. Society for Latin American Anthropology Publication Series, no. 10. Washington, DC: Society for Latin American Anthropology.

Chibnik, Michael. 2001. "Oaxacan Wood Carvers: Global Markets and Local Work Organizations." In *Plural Globalities in Multiple Localities: New World Borders,* ed. M. W. Rees and J. Smart, pp. 129–148. Lanham, MD: University Press of America.

———. 2003. *Crafting Tradition: The Making and Marketing of Oaxacan Wood Carvings.* Austin: University of Texas Press.

Chiñas, Beverly. 1993. *La Zanduga: Of Fieldwork and Friendship in Southern Mexico.* Prospect Heights, IL: Waveland Press.

Cohen, Jeffrey H. 1998. "Craft Production and the Challenge of the Global Market: An Artisans' Cooperative in Oaxaca, Mexico." *Human Organization* 57(1): 74–82.

———. 1999. *Cooperation and Community: Economy and Society in Oaxaca.* Austin: University of Texas Press.

———. 2001. "Transnational Migration in Rural Oaxaca, Mexico: Dependency, Development, and the Household." *American Anthropologist* 103(4): 954–967.

———. 2002. "Social Responses to Migration among Mexican Ethnic Minorities: Outcomes in Sending and Receiving Communities." AMID Working Paper Series 3/2002. Aalborg: Academy for Migration Studies in Denmark.

Cohen, Jeffrey H., Alicia Silvia Gijón-Cruz, Rafael G. Reyes-Morales, and Garry Chick. 2003. "A Local Approach to the Study of Transnational Processes: Survey Ethnography in the Central Valley of Oaxaca, Mexico." *Field Methods* 15(4): 366–385.

CONAPO (Consejo Nacional de Población). 2000. *Carpetas informativas, retos demográficos 2000: La población, un desafío permanente.* http://www.conapo.gob.mx/relevante/reto2000.htm (accessed November 8, 2001).

Conway, Dennis. 2000. "Notions Unbound: A Critical (Re)Reading of Transnationalism Suggests That U.S.-Caribbean Circuits Tell the Story Better." In *Theoretical and Methodological Issues in Migration Research: Interdisciplinary, Intergenera-*

tional, and International Perspectives, ed. B. Agozino, pp. 203–226. Aldershot, UK: Ashgate.

Conway, Dennis, and Jeffrey H. Cohen. 1998. "Consequences of Return Migration and Remittances for Mexican Transnational Communities." *Economic Geography* 74(1): 26–44.

———. 2002. "Local Dynamics in Multi-Local, Transnational Spaces of Rural Mexico: Oaxacan Experiences." *International Journal of Population Geography* 9(1): 141–161.

Cook, Scott, and Leigh Binford. 1990. *Obliging Need: Rural Petty Industry in Mexican Capitalism.* Austin: University of Texas Press.

Cook, Scott, and M. Diskin. 1976. *Markets in Oaxaca.* Austin: University of Texas Press.

Corbett, Jack A., Murad A. Musalem Merhy, Othon C. Ríos Vázquez, and Héctor A. Vázquez Hernandez, eds. 1992. *Migración y etnicidad en Oaxaca.* Vanderbilt University Publications in Anthropology, no. 43. Nashville.

Cornelius, Wayne A., and Jorge A. Bustamante, eds. 1989. *Mexican Migration to the United States: Origins, Consequences, and Policy Options.* La Jolla, CA: Center for U.S.-Mexican Studies, University of California, San Diego.

Craig, John G. 1993. *The Nature of Co-operation.* New York: Black Rose Books.

Craig, Richard B. 1971. *The Bracero Program: Interest Groups and Foreign Policy.* Austin: University of Texas Press.

Curran, Sara R., and Estela Rivero-Fuentes. 2003. "Engendering Migrant Networks: The Case of Mexican Migration." *Demography* 40(2): 289–307.

de la Garza, Rodolfo O., and Manuel Orozco. 2002. "Binational Impact of Latino Remittances." In *Sending Money Home: Hispanic Remittances and Community Development,* ed. R. O. de la Garza and B. L. Lowell, pp. 29–51. Lanham, MD: Rowman and Littlefield.

DeWalt, Billie R., Martha W. Rees, and Arthur D. Murphy. 1994. *The End of Agrarian Reform in Mexico: Past Lessons, Future Prospects.* La Jolla, CA: Center for U.S.-Mexico Studies, University of California, San Diego.

Diaz Briquets, Sergio. 1991. "The Effects of International Migration on Latin America." In *The Unsettled Relationship: Labor Migration and Economic Development,* ed. D. G. Papademetriou and P. L. Martin, pp. 183–200. Westport, CT: Greenwood Press.

DIGEPO (Dirección General de Población de Oaxaca). 1999. *Oaxaca, indicadores socioeconómicos índice y grado en marginación por localidad (1995).* Oaxaca: Dirección General de Población de Oaxaca y el Consejo Nacional de Población.

Donato, Katherine M. 1993. "Current Trends and Patterns of Female Migration: Evidence from Mexico." *International Migration Review* 27(4): 748–768.

Downing, Theodore E. 1979. "Explaining Migration in Mexico and Elsewhere." In *Migration across Frontiers: Mexico and the United States,* ed. F. Camara and R. Van Kemper, pp. 159–167. Contributions of the Latin American Anthropology Group, vol. 3. Albany: State University of New York.

Durand, Jorge, and Douglas S. Massey. 1992. "Mexican Migration to the United States: A Critical Review." *Latin American Research Review* 27(2): 3–42.

Durand, Jorge, Emilio A. Parrado, and Douglas S. Massey. 1996a. "International Migration and Development in Mexican Communities." *Demography* 33(2): 249–264.

———. 1996b. "Migradollars and Development: A Reconsideration of the Mexican Case." *International Migration Review* 30(2): 423–444.

Durand, Jorge, Douglas S. Massey, and Fernando Charvet. 2000. "The Changing Geography of Mexican Immigration to the United States: 1910–1996." *Social Science Quarterly* 81(1): 1–15.

Durrenburger, E. Paul, and Nicola Tannenbaum. 2002. "Chayanov and Theory in Economic Anthropology." In *Theory in Economic Anthropology,* ed. J. Ensminger, pp. 137–153. Society for Economic Anthropology Monograph 18. Walnut Creek, CA: AltaMira Press.

Embriz, Arnulfo. 1993. *Indicadores socioeconómicos de los pueblos indígenas de México, 1990*. Mexico City: Dirección de Investigación y Promoción Cultural, Subdirección de Investigación, Instituto Nacional Indigenista.

Faist, Thomas. 1997. "The Crucial Meso-Level." In *International Migration, Immobility, and Development: Multidisciplinary Perspectives,* ed. T. Hammar, G. Brochmann, K. Tamas, and T. Faist, pp. 187–218. New York: Berg.

Fischer, Peter A., Reiner Martin, and Thomas Staubhaar. 1997. "Should I Stay or Should I Go?" In *International Migration, Immobility, and Development: Multidisciplinary Perspectives,* ed. T. Hammar, G. Brochmann, K. Tamas, and T. Faist, pp. 49–90. New York: Berg.

Folbre, Nancy. 1988. "The Black Four of Hearts: Towards a New Paradigm of Household Economics." In *A Home Divided: Women and Income in the Third World,* ed. D. Dwyer and J. Bruce, pp. 248–262. Stanford, CA: Stanford University Press.

Fortes, Meyer. 1971. Introduction to *The Development Cycle in Domestic Groups,* ed. J. Goody, pp. 1–15. Cambridge: Cambridge University Press.

Foster, George M. 1979. *Tzintzuntzan: Mexican Peasants in a Changing World.* New York: Elsevier.

Fox, Jonathan, and Josefina Aranda. 1996. *Decentralization and Rural Development in Mexico: Community Participation in Oaxaca's Municipal Funds Program.* La Jolla, CA: Center for U.S.-Mexican Studies, University of California, San Diego.

Gamio, Manuel. 1931. *The Mexican Immigrant: His Life Story.* Chicago: University of Chicago Press.

García de León, Antonio. 2003. *Otro ratito no más: Los sones de México.* Compact disc, Discos Corasón COR 801. http://www.corason.com/.

Gledhill, John. 1995. *Neoliberalism, Transnationalization, and Rural Poverty: A Case Study of Michoacán, Mexico.* Boulder, CO: Westview Press.

Goldring, Luin. 1998. "The Power of Status in Transnational Social Fields." In *Transnationalism from Below,* ed. M. P. Smith and L. E. Guarnizo, vol. 6 of *Compara-*

tive Urban Community Research, pp. 165–195. New Brunswick, NJ: Transaction Publishers.
Greenacre, Michael J. 1984. *Theory and Applications of Correspondence Analysis.* London: Academic Press.
Greenberg, James B. 1995. "Capital, Ritual, and Boundaries of the Closed Corporate Community." In *Articulating Hidden Histories,* ed. R. Rapp and J. Schneider, pp. 67–81. Berkeley and Los Angeles: University of California Press.
Guidi, Marta. 1993. "¿Es realmente la migración una estrategia de supervivencia? Un ejemplo en la Mixteca Alta Oaxaqueña." *Revista Internacional de Sociología Tercera Epoca,* no. 5: 89–109.
Hammar, Tomas, and Kristof Tamas. 1997. "Why Do People Go or Stay?" In *International Migration, Immobility, and Development: Multidisciplinary Perspectives,* ed. T. Hammar, G. Brochmann, K. Tamas, and T. Faist, pp. 1–20. New York: Berg.
Helweg, A. W. 1983. "Emigrant Remittances: Their Nature and Impact on a Punjabi Village." *New Community* 10: 67–84.
Heyman, Josiah M. 1998. *Finding a Moral Heart for U.S. Immigration Policy: An Anthropological Perspective.* Washington, DC: American Anthropological Association.
Hirabayashi, Lane Ryo. 1983. "On the Formation of Migrant Village Associations in Mexico: Mixtec and Mountain Zapotec in Mexico City." *Urban Anthropology* 12(1): 29–44.
———. 1993. *Cultural Capital: Mountain Zapotec Migrant Associations in Mexico City.* Tucson: University of Arizona Press.
Hirschman, Albert O. 1970. *Exit, Voice, and Loyalty: Responses to Decline in Firms, Organizations, and States.* Cambridge, MA: Harvard University Press.
Howell, Jayne. 1999. "Expanding Women's Roles in Southern Mexico: Educated, Employed Oaxaquenas." *Journal of Anthropological Research* 55(1): 99–127.
Hulshof, Marje. 1991. *Zapotec Moves: Networks and Remittances of U.S. Bound Migrants from Oaxaca, Mexico.* Amsterdam: University of Amsterdam.
INEGI (Instituto Nacional de Estadística Geografía e Informática). 1999. *Imágenes económicas del estado de Oaxaca.* Aguascalientes, Aguascalientes, Mexico: INEGI.
———. 2001a. *Anuario estadístico Oaxaca.* Vol. 2. Aguascalientes, Aguascalientes, Mexico: INEGI.
———. 2001b. *Distribución porcentual de la población por características migratorias según entidad federativa, 1995.* http://www.inegi.gob.mx/estadistica/espanol/sociodem/fsociodemografia.html (accessed October 8, 2001).
———. 2002a. *XII censo general de población y vivienda 2000.* Aguascalientes, Aguascalientes, Mexico: INEGI.
———. 2002b. *XII censo general de población y vivienda 2000: Síntesis de resultados Estados Unidos Mexicanos.* http://www.inegi.gob.mx/difusion/espanol/poblacion/definitivos/nal/sintesis/migracion.pdf (accessed February 18, 2002).
Iszaevich, Abraham. 1988. "Migración campesina del Valle de Oaxaca." In *Migración en el Occidente de México,* ed. G. Lopez-Castro, pp. 187–199. Zamora, Michoacán: Colegio de Michoacán.

Jones, Richard C. 1998. "Introduction: The Renewed Role of Remittances in the New World Order." *Economic Geography* 74(1): 1–7.

Kearney, Michael. 1994. "Desde el indigenismo a los derechos humanos: Etnicidad y política más allá de la Mixteca." *Nueva Antropología* 14(46): 49–67.

———. 1995. "The Effects of Transnational Culture, Economy, and Migration on Mixtec Identity in Oaxacalifornia." In *The Bubbling Cauldron: Race, Ethnicity, and the Urban Crisis,* ed. M. P. Smith and J. R. Feagin, pp. 226–243. Minneapolis: University of Minnesota Press.

———. 1996. *Reconceptualizing the Peasantry: Anthropology in Global Perspective.* Boulder, CO: Westview Press.

———. 2000. "Transnational Oaxacan Indigenous Identity: The Case of Mixtecs and Zapotecs." *Identities* 7(2): 173–195.

Keely, Charles B. 2000. "Demography and International Migration." In *Migration Theory,* ed. J. F. Hollifield, pp. 43–60. New York: Routledge.

Kowalewski, Stephen A., and Jacqueline J. Saindon. 1992. "The Spread of Literacy in a Latin American Peasant Society: Oaxaca, 1890–1980." *Comparative Studies in Society and History* 34(1): 110–141.

Leslie, Charles M. 1960. *Now We Are Civilized: A Study of the World View of the Zapotec Indians of Mitla, Oaxaca.* Detroit: Wayne State University Press.

Levitt, Peggy. 1998. "Social Remittances: Migration Driven Local-Level Forms of Cultural Diffusion." *International Migration Review* 32(4): 926–948.

Lowell, Briant Lindsey, and Rodolfo O. de la Garza. 2002. "The Development Role of Remittances in U.S. Latino Communities and Latin America." In *Sending Money Home: Hispanic Remittances and Community Development,* ed. R. O. de la Garza and B. L. Lowell, pp. 3–27. Lanham, MD: Rowman and Littlefield.

Lozano Ascencio, Fernando. 1993. *Bringing It Back Home: Remittances to Mexico from Migrant Workers in the United States.* Trans. A. Yáñez. La Jolla, CA: Center for U.S.-Mexican Studies, University of California, San Diego.

———. 1998. "Las remesas de los migrantes mexicanos en Estados Unidos: Estimaciones para 1995." In *Migration between Mexico and the United States,* vol. 3, pp. 1189–1214. Austin, TX: Mexican Ministry of Foreign Affairs and the U.S. Commission on Immigration Reform.

Magagnini, Stephen. 2002. "Radio Gives Mixtecs Their Own Voice: 'La Hora Mixteca' Reaches Out across California." *Sacramento (CA) Bee,* October 20, 2002. http://www.sacbee.com/.

Marcelli, Enrico A., and Wayne A. Cornelius. 2001. "The Changing Profile of Mexican Migrants to the United States: New Evidence from California and Mexico." *Latin American Research Review* 36(3):105–131.

Martin, Philip L. 1991. "Labor Migration: Theory and Reality." In *The Unsettled Relationship: Labor Migration and Economic Development,* ed. D. G. Papademetriou and P. L. Martin, pp. 27–42. Westport, CT: Greenwood Press.

———. 1996. "Mexico: Polls, Remittances, and Economy." *Migration News.* http://

migration.ucdavis.edu/mn/more.php?id=1046_0_2_0 (accessed November 17, 2003).

Massey, Douglas S. 1987. *Return to Aztlan: The Social Process of International Migration from Western Mexico.* Berkeley and Los Angeles: University of California Press.

———. 1990. "Social Structure, Household Strategies, and the Cumulative Causation of Migration." *Population Index* 56(1): 3–26.

Massey, Douglas S., Joaquin Arango, Graeme Hugo, Ali Kouaouci, Adela Pellegrino, and J. Edward Taylor. 1993. "Theories of International Migration: A Review and Appraisal." *Population and Development* 19(3): 431–466.

———. 1998. *Worlds in Motion: Understanding International Migration at the End of the Millennium.* New York: Oxford University Press.

Massey, Douglas S., Luin Goldring, and Jorge Durand. 1994. "Continuities in Transnational Migration: An Analysis of Nineteen Mexican Communities." *American Journal of Sociology* 99(6): 1492–1533.

McArthur, Harold J., Jr. 1979. "The Effects of Overseas Work on Return Migrants and Their Home Communities: The Philippines Case." *Papers in Anthropology* 20: 85–104.

Mendieta y Núñez, Lucio. 1960. *Efectos sociales de la reforma agraria en tres comunidades ejidales de la república mexicana.* Mexico City: Universidad Nacional Autónoma de México.

Meyer, Birgit, and Peter Geschiere. 1999. Introduction *to Globalization and Identity: Dialects of Flow and Closure,* ed. B. Meyer and P. Geschiere, pp. 1–15. Malden, MA: Blackwell Publishers.

Mills, M. E. 1993. "We Are Not Like Our Mothers: Migration, Modernity, and Identity in Northeast Thailand." PhD diss., University of California, Berkeley.

Mines, Richard, and Douglas S. Massey. 1985. "Patterns of Migration to the United States from Two Mexican Communities." *Latin American Research Review* 20(2): 104–123.

Mitchell, Don. 1995. "There's No Such Thing as Culture: Towards a Reconceptualization of the Idea of Culture in Geography." *Transactions of the Institute of British Geographers* 20(1): 102–116.

Mittelman, James H. 2000. *The Globalization Syndrome: Transformation and Resistance.* Princeton, NJ: Princeton University Press.

Monto, Alexander. 1994. *The Roots of Mexican Labor Migration.* Westport, CT: Praeger.

Moore, Henrietta L. 1988. *Feminism and Anthropology.* Oxford: Polity Press.

Mountz, Alison, and Richard Wright. 1996. "Daily Life in the Transnational Migrant Community of San Agustín, Oaxaca, and Poughkeepsie, New York." *Diaspora* 5(3): 403–428.

Murphy, Arthur D., and A. Stepick. 1991. *Social Inequality in Oaxaca: A History of Resistance and Change.* Philadelphia: Temple University Press.

Mutersbaugh, Tad. 2002. "Migration, Common Property, and Communal Labor:

Cultural Politics and Agency in a Mexican Village." *Political Geography* 21(4): 473–494.

Nader, Laura. 1969. "The Zapotec of Oaxaca." In *Handbook of Middle American Indians,* ed. R. Wauchope, pp. 329–359. Austin: University of Texas Press.

———. 1990. *Harmony Ideology: Justice and Control in a Zapotec Mountain Village.* Stanford, CA: Stanford University Press.

Nangengast, Carole, Rudolfo Stavenhagen, and Michael Kearney. 1992. *Human Rights and Indigenous Workers: The Mixtecs in Mexico and the United States.* La Jolla, CA: Center for U.S.-Mexican Studies, San Diego.

Netting, Robert M., Richard Wilk, and Eric Arnould, eds. 1984. *Households: Comparative and Historical Studies of the Domestic Group.* Berkeley and Los Angeles: University of California Press.

Nutini, Hugo. 1984. *Ritual Kinship: Ideological and Structural Integration of the Compadrazgo System in Rural Tlaxcala.* Vol. 2. Princeton, NJ: Princeton University Press.

Orozco, Manuel. 2002. "Latino Hometown Associations as Agents of Development in Latin America." In *Sending Money Home: Hispanic Remittances and Community Development,* ed. R. O. de la Garza and B. L. Lowell, pp. 85–99. Lanham, MD: Rowman and Littlefield.

Otero, Gerardo. 1996. *Neoliberalism Revisited: Economic Restructuring and Mexico's Political Future.* Boulder, CO: Westview Press.

———. 1999. *Farewell to the Peasantry? Political Class Formation in Rural Mexico.* Boulder, CO: Westview Press.

Papademetriou, Demetrios G. 1991. "Migration and Development: The Unsettled Relationship." In *The Unsettled Relationship: Labor Migration and Economic Development,* ed. D. G. Papademetriou and P. L. Martin, pp. 213–221. Westport, CT: Greenwood Press.

Pennartz, Paul. J., and Anke Niehof. 1999. *The Domestic Domain: Chances, Choices and Strategies of Family Households.* Aldershot, UK: Ashgate.

Ponce de León, Dolores. 2002. Bracero Justice Project. http://bracerojustice.com/main.htm (accessed September 10, 2002).

Portes, Alejandro, Luis Eduardo Guarnizo, and William J. Haller. 2002. "Transnational Entrepreneurs: An Alternative Form of Immigrant Economic Adaptation." *American Sociological Review* 67: 278–298.

Ravenstein, E. G. 1889. "The Laws of Migration." *Journal of the Royal Statistical Society* 52(2): 241–301.

Rees, Martha W., and Dolores Coronel Ortiz. 2002. "From Tapachula to LA: Female Migration in the Central Valleys of Oaxaca, Mexico, 1950–1998." Unpublished manuscript.

Reichert, Joshua. 1981. "The Migrant Syndrome: Seasonal U.S. Wage Labor and Rural Development in Central Mexico." *Human Organization* 40(1): 56–66.

Reichert, Joshua, and Douglas S. Massey. 1980. "History and Trends in U.S.-Bound Migration from a Mexican Town." *International Migration Review* 14(4): 475–491.

Rempel, Henry, and Richard A. Lobdell. 1978. "The Role of Urban-to-Rural Remittances in Rural Development." *Journal of Development Studies* 14: 324–341.

Rivera-Salgado, Gaspar. 1999. "Mixtec Activism in Oaxacalifornia." *American Behavioral Scientist* 42(9): 1439–1458.

Royce, Anya P. 1981. "Isthmus Zapotec Households: Economic Responses to Scarcity and Abundance." *Urban Anthropology* 10(3): 269–286.

Rubenstein, Hymie. 1992. "Migration, Development, and Remittances in Rural Mexico." *International Migration/Migraciones Internacionales* 30(2): 127–153.

Runsten, David, and Michael Kearney. 1994. *A Survey of Oaxacan Village Networks in California Agriculture.* Davis, CA: California Institute for Rural Studies.

Russell, Sharon Staton. 1992. "Migrant Remittances and Development." *International Migration/Migraciones Internacionales* 30(3/4): 267–287.

Selby, Henry A. 1974. *Zapotec Deviance: The Convergence of Folk and Modern Sociology.* Austin: University of Texas Press.

SEN (Secretaria de la Economía Nacional). 1953. *Séptimo censo de población, 1950.* Mexico City: SEN.

Shankman, Paul. 1976. *Migration and Underdevelopment: The Case of Western Samoa.* Boulder, CO: Westview Press.

Smith, James F., and Ken Ellingwood. 2001. "Sept. 11 Leaves Carpet Loomers Idle in Oaxacan Town." *Los Angeles Times,* November 28.

Smith, Robert C. 1998. "Transnational Localities: Community, Technology, and the Politics of Membership within the Context of Mexico and U.S. Migration." In *Transnationalism from Below,* ed. M. P. Smith and L. E. Guarnizo, vol. 6 of *Comparative Urban Community Research,* pp. 196–238. New Brunswick, NJ: Transaction Publishers.

Stark, Oded, and J. Edward Taylor. 1986. "Testing for Relative Deprivation: Mexican Labor Migration." Migration and Development Program, Harvard University, Discussion Paper no. 26. Center for Population Studies, Cambridge, MA.

Stark, Oded, and Shlomo Yitzhaki. 1988. "Labour Migration as a Response to Relative Deprivation." *Journal of Population Economics* 1(1): 57–70.

Stephen, Lynn. 1991. *Zapotec Women.* Austin: University of Texas Press.

Stuart, James, and Michael Kearney. 1981. "Causes and Effects of Agricultural Labor Migration from the Mixteca of Oaxaca to California." Working Paper no. 28. La Jolla, CA: Center for U.S.-Mexican Studies, University of California, San Diego.

Taylor, J. Edward. 1992. "Remittances and Inequality Reconsidered: Direct, Indirect, and Intertemporal Effects." *Journal of Policy Modeling* 14(2): 187–208.

———. 1999. "The New Economics of Labor Migration and the Role of Remittances in the Migration Process." *International Migration/Migraciones Internacionales* 37(1): 63–88.

Taylor, J. Edward, Joaquin Arango, Graeme Hugo, Ali Kouaouci, Douglas S. Massey, and Adela Pellegrino. 1996a. "International Migration and Community Development." *Population Index* 62(3): 397–418.

———. 1996b. "International Migration and National Development." *Population Index* 62(2): 181–212.

Thorner, D., B. Kerblay, and R. E. F. Smith, eds. 1966. *A. V. Chayanov on the Theory of Peasant Economy.* Homewood, IL: Richard D. Irwin, for the American Economic Association.

Van Hook, Jennifer, and Frank D. Bean. 1998. "Estimating Unauthorized Mexican Migration to the United States: Issues and Results." In *Migration between Mexico and the United States,* vol. 2, pp. 511–550. Austin, TX: Mexican Ministry of Foreign Affairs and the U.S. Commission on Immigration Reform.

Verduzco, Gustavo, and Kurt Unger. 1998. "Impacts of Migration in Mexico." In *Migration between Mexico and the United States,* vol. 1, pp. 395–435. Austin, TX: Mexican Ministry of Foreign Affairs and the U.S. Commission on Immigration Reform.

Verduzco Igartúa, Gustavo. 1995. "La migración mexicana a Estados Unidos: Recuento de un proceso histórico." *Estudios Sociológicos* 13(39): 573–594.

Warman, Arturo. 1978. "Política agraria o política agricola." *Comercio Exterior* 28(6): 681–687.

Watanabe, John M. 1992. *Maya Saints and Souls in a Changing World.* Austin: University of Texas Press.

Weller, Susan C., and A. Kimball Romney. 1990. *Metric Scaling: Correspondence Analysis.* Newbury Park, CA: Sage.

Wheelock, Jane. 1992. "The Household in the Total Economy." In *Real-Life Economics: Understanding Wealth Creation,* ed. P. Ekins and M. Max-Neef, pp. 123–136. New York: Routledge.

Wiest, Raymond E. 1973. "Wage-Labor Migration and the Household in a Mexican Town." *Journal of Anthropological Research* 29(3): 180–209.

Wilk, Richard R. 1989. "Decision Making and Resource Flows within the Household: Beyond the Black Box." In *The Household Economy,* ed. R. R. Wilk, pp. 23–54. Boulder, CO: Westview Press.

———. 1991. *Household Ecology: Economic Change and Domestic Life among the Kekchi Maya in Belize.* Tucson: University of Arizona Press.

Wilson, Tamar Diana. 2000. "Anti-immigrant Sentiment and the Problem of Reproduction/Maintenance in Mexican Immigration to the United States." *Critique of Anthropology* 20(2): 191–213.

Wolpert, Julian. 1964. "The Decision Process in a Spatial Context." *Annals of the Association of American Geographers* 54: 537–558.

Zlolniski, Christian. 2001. *Immigrant Labor in the New United States Economy: An Anthropological Critique.* Milwaukee: Society for Economic Anthropology.

INDEX